LIVING IN THE KINGDOM

0-8066-4998-4 John McCullough Bade
Will I Sing Again? Listening for the Melody of Grace in the Silence of Illness and Loss

0-8066-4988-7 Richard F. Bansemer
Getting Ready for the New Life: Facing Illness or Death with the Word and Prayers

0-8066-4991-7 D. Michael Bennethum
Listen! God Is Calling! Luther Speaks of Vocation, Faith, and Work

0-8066-4935-6 David A. Brondos
The Letter and the Spirit: Discerning God's Will in a Complex World

0-8066-5174-1 Eric Burtness
Leading on Purpose: Intentionality and Teaming in Congregational Life

0-8066-4992-5 Michael L. Cooper-White
On a Wing and a Prayer: Faithful Leadership in the 21st Century

0-8066-4995-X Barbara DeGrote-Sorensen & David Allen Sorensen
Let the Servant Church Arise!

0-8066-4936-4 Robert Driver-Bishop
People of Purpose: 40 Life Lessons from the New Testament

0-8066-4999-2 Rochelle Melander & Harold Eppley
Our Lives Are Not Our Own: Saying "Yes" to God

0-8066-5161-X Norma Cook Everist
Open the Doors and See All the People: Stories of Church Identity and Vocation

0-8066-4596-2 Kelly A. Fryer
Reclaiming the "L" Word: Renewing the Church from Its Lutheran Core

0-8066-4989-5 Ann E. Hafften
Water from the Rock: Lutheran Voices from Palestine

0-8066-4990-9 Susan K. Hedahl
Who Do You Say That I Am? 21st Century Preaching

0-8066-4997-6 Mary E. Hinkle
Signs of Belonging: Luther's Marks of the Church and the Christian Life

0-8066-5172-5 Robert F. Holley & Paul E. Walters
Called by God to Serve: Reflections for Church Leaders

0-8066-4994-1 Martin E. Marty
Speaking of Trust: Conversing with Luther about the Sermon on the Mount

0-8066-4987-9 Cynthia Moe-Lobeda
Public Church: For the Life of the World

0-8066-4996-8 Carolyn Coon Mowchan & Damian Anthony Vraniak
Connecting with God in a Disconnected World: A Guide for Spiritual Growth and Renewal

0-8066-4993-3 Craig L. Nessan
Give Us This Day: A Lutheran Proposal for Ending World Hunger

0-8066-5111-3 William Russell
Praying for Reform: Luther, Prayer, and the Christian Life

0-8066-5173-3 Joseph Sittler
Gravity and Grace: Reflections and Provocations

See www.lutheranvoices.com

LIVING IN THE KINGDOM
Reflections on Luther's Catechism
Revised Edition

Alvin N. Rogness

Augsburg Fortress

Minneapolis

LIVING IN THE KINGDOM
Reflections on Luther's Catechism
Revised Edition

Original volume prepared under the auspices of the Division for Life and Mission in the Congregation and the Board of Publication of the American Lutheran Church. Copyright © 1976 Augsburg Publishing House.

Large-quantity purchases or custom editions of these books are available at a discount from the publisher. For more information, contact the sales department at Augsburg Fortress, Publishers, 1-800-328-4648, or write to: Sales Director, Augsburg Fortress, Publishers, P.O. Box 1209, Minneapolis, MN 55440-1209.

Direct Scripture quotations are from New Revised Standard Version Bible, copyright © 1989 Division of Christian Education of the National Council of the Churches of Christ in the United States of America. Used by permission.

Catechism quotations are from The Small Catechism in Contemporary English, copyright 1968 by Augsburg Publishing House, the Board of Publication of the Lutheran Church in America, and Concordia Publishing House; used by permission.

Editor: Scott Tunseth; Cover Design: © Koechel Peterson and Associates, Inc., Minneapolis, MN www.koechelpeterson.com and Diana Running; Cover Photo: Copyright Getty Images / Photodisc

Library of Congress Cataloging-in-Publication Data
Rogness, Alvin N., 1906-
  Living in the Kingdom : reflections on Luther's Catechism / Alvin N. Rogness—Rev. ed.
    p. cm.— (Lutheran voices)
  ISBN 0-8066-4934-8 (pbk. : alk. paper)
  1. Luther, Martin, 1483-1546. Kleine Katechismus. 2. Lutheran Church—Catechisms—English. I. Title. II. Series.

  BX8070.L8R59 2005
  238'.41—dc22   2005013846

The paper used in this publication meets the minimum requirements of American National Standard for Information Sciences—Permanence of Paper for Printed Library Materials, ANSI Z329.48-1984. ♾ ™

Manufactured in the U.S.A.

09   08   07   06   05   1   2   3   4   5   6   7   8   9   10

Contents

Foreword

The writer of this volume, Alvin Rogness, was our father.

Dad was born in 1906. He was the oldest of six children. In 1919, when he was thirteen, his father was gravely ill. The flu epidemic had not bypassed the small town of Astoria, South Dakota, and everyone knew that this was a matter of life and death. Over the years, Dad returned to the memory of those dark days to share a pivotal moment. Terrified by the thought that his father might not live, and feeling the burden of being the oldest child, he went to his own mother for reassurance. "What will happen to us if Father dies?" His mother, Mina, reached out to him, took her in his arms, and said, "God will take care of us. We will be all right."

In much the same way, the five of us learned the faith at home, from him, and from our mother. We learned it daily, in their teaching and living, in their devotions and their conversation; we learned it in living with them through the death of our brother Paul at age twenty-four. All of life was grounded in the knowledge that it all came from God, and we would all return to God. During the years we had on this earth we were living in the kingdom—a much broader kingdom than simply our years here.

Living in the Kingdom was originally written as a companion to Luther's Small Catechism, which was at the time the backbone of confirmation instruction. Generations came to find Luther's to-the-point explanations of the Ten Commandments, the Creed, the Lord's Prayer, and description of the sacraments and ministry to be a wonderful summary of the faith. Lutheran hymnals in this country until 1959 (when the "red book" came out) contained the Small Catechism and the Augsburg Confession; this served the dual purpose of reminding us of the central teachings of Lutheran theology, and providing a resource for wandering minds during any worship that might have been less than inspiring.

The catechism was meant for the home. After a while, however, the church became nervous about the Apostle Paul's warning against partaking in Holy Communion "without understanding," (at peril of their eternal souls) and relegated the teaching of the faith to the clergy to be assured of proper doctrine being in place before one became a full communicant. Thereafter, the catechism was taught at church to seventh and eighth graders who were preparing for their entrance into church membership and participation in Holy Communion.

For three of us—Michael, Stephen, and Martha—Dad was our confirmation teacher. It might be nice to tell some stories about the hugely profound impact of those class sessions. When we reached back for memories of that instruction, however, we came up with things far more mundane. Stephen recalls always having to sit up front (have the pastor's kids always been among the most squir-relly?… or is it because, as Martha remembers, the pastor's kid is going to feel pressure to not be a prude!). Martha remembers being seated alphabetically next to John Rogers, on whom she had a huge crush and from whom she had to be regularly separated by her teacher/pastor/father. Stephen also remembers the terror of what was called the public catechization, but he remembers it as an inquisition, where the congregation looked far more like a judge and jury than parents and relatives. Now-seminary-professor Michael thinks back and wonders if maybe Dad's purpose for that public questioning was to shame the parents with the realization that their children knew things they didn't, and should! Regardless, it drove home the point that there were things about God and faith that were worth know-ing. We suppose confirmation instruction was perhaps too focused on "head knowledge," but the result was that we knew some impor-tant things about the Bible, the faith, and the life of the church.

Two impressions stand out, and relate directly to the purpose of this book.

First, faith ushered us into a group. It wasn't a doctrinal propo-sition that was left to individual choice. For confirmation students, it meant being part of a class of kids who had a niche in the life of their church whether they happened to be popular or not. And if everyone hung in, all were confirmed—no grades, no distinctions. We were part of a larger whole. Educationally it can be debated whether confirmation age is the best time for instruction or not, but it is not simply dogma that's at issue here. We are as much *socialized* into the body of Christ as *taught* into it! More than the knowledge gained, Martha is left remembering that she found great security and acceptance in the simple fact that all of her friends and class-mates were at *our* church—together—learning about our faith, not math or science. Somehow that made it "OK" to be a Christian, to be going to church, to go on retreats. Together. We learned "com-munity" because it was how we learned about the faith.

Second, and perhaps most importantly, for Dad the matters of faith were always a give-and-take between truths we held and ques-tions that swirled. Dad's study was a room of warmth in our house, not simply because of the ever-present pipe smoke, but because the minute any of us would wander in and plop ourselves down on the couch, he was ours, ready to muse and listen and wonder with us. This was the faith—the questions and mystery and unknown-ness of it. As a parish pastor, the older kids remember his regular gather-ings of college students for discussion of faith and ministry. In his parish years at Ames, Iowa, one of those students was Kent Knutson, later professor at Luther Seminary, president of Wartburg Seminary, and, before his untimely death, president of the American Lutheran Church. There were hundreds of others. So it's fitting this little volume is written largely in question-and-answer format. A lively faith is never doctrinaire, but is always made up of a healthy amount of both questions and answers.

We offer these memories to underscore how trust in a loving God has, for us, taken root in our hearts through the love and care of fam-ily and friends. We children of Alvin and Nora Rogness know the gift of love through which God binds us all. That love is woven through his writings, in his preaching, and in the many encounters of grace that people have shared with us over the years. We have a God who holds us in love, and who will not let us go. Even when tragedy and heartaches would come, as they will for everyone, the enduring love of God that Dad experienced in his mother's arms, and that we experi-enced from him, have kept us steadfastly living in the kingdom.

The children of Alvin Rogness—Michael, Stephen, Martha (Vetter), Peter, and Andrew

Introduction

What does it mean in terms of daily living for a person to be a responsible citizen of God's kingdom? How do the teachings of the Bible and the church help one to meet the often perplexing problems of life? For generations, people have found help in dealing with such questions in Martin Luther's Small Catechism. Its timeless truths speak to any age, but they gain added value when they are specifically applied to each succeeding generation in our changing world.

To make such application for our day is the aim of this book. On the assumption that our actions and attitudes ultimately depend on what we believe, it seeks to help present day readers clarify their beliefs and apply them to life in today's world. This study is equally valuable for young people and adults and can be carried out in classes, homes, or individual reading.

A note about the language for God in this edition

When this volume was written and edited in 1976, the male pronoun was used for God as a standard practice. Some of the occurrences of such usage have been changed in this revised edition, but the editors decided not to eliminate the male pronoun as a general rule, as this would change the straightforward nature of Rogness' original text.

Using Luther's Small Catechism

This book does not contain the full text of Luther's Small Catechism. See the final page of this book for options, should you wish to use the Small Catechism alongside *Living in the Kingdom*.

1

Let's Talk about You

In this book we will talk about many things. First, let's talk about you.

You are a remarkable person, because God made you and because he loves you. In Baptism, God enrolls you in the greatest family on earth, the holy Christian church. In this great company God comforts you, guides you, and strengthens you. When death is done with you, God puts you on your feet again in another and more wonderful part of his vast empire. You belong to God, as a son or daughter. God wants you forever.

You also belong to other people, especially to your family. In a sense you also belong to friends. And you belong to a country as a citizen.

Biologists tell you that you belong to the family of animals. You are a mammal. You resemble the animals, even fish. But you are different. No animal builds airplanes or writes letters to friends.

As a human being, you belong to the human family. Unlike all other animals and birds, you have been given the gift of choice. You decide matters: what is right and wrong, for instance. Animals and fish and birds do things by instinct alone. Not you. God gave you freedom to choose between good and evil, to obey him or to disobey him.

This wonderful gift of freedom that God gave us has been the source of much trouble. Beginning with Adam and Eve, the people of this earth have a long record of choosing evil instead of good, of disobeying God instead of obeying him. Almost all the sadness on this earth, like wars and crime, is the direct result of our disobedience. Even hunger and disease are often the result of ignoring the will of God.

In any event, you live in a world that will challenge you with many difficult choices and problems. It is not an easy life. You are not on vacation.

But don't be depressed. God has given you a brain to think with and a will to choose with. God honors you with important tasks to do.

God gives you clear clues as to what he wants you to do. And best of all, God promises to be with you all the way. When you fail him, God will forgive you and give you a new start.

We must not forget the hundreds of millions of people throughout history who have been caught up in God's will and whose lives have done much to make the world a better place. The history of the world is not one of continuous failure. There is much nobility, much compassion, and much decency among countless people. God is at work in us, whenever we let him.

God loves you. And there is only one you. No one on earth is just like you. God has his eye on you. Whatever your abilities are, he can use you, often in more wonderful ways than you dare to think.

The earth is a wonderful place, too. In spite of much sorrow and hurt, the earth has beauty and goodness. You can be God's agent to give it more beauty and goodness.

Why did God bother to create us?

Maybe God was lonely, or wanted someone with whom he could share his blessings (see Isaiah 43:7). Whatever else moved God to create people, one thing is clear from the Bible: he created us because he loves us (see Ephesians 1:3-5).

Couldn't God have kept human beings from bringing misery into the world?

Not unless God had taken away our freedom. If God had decided to make us like other animals or had given us instinct only for good, he could have kept us from war and crime. But that would be like locking us up to keep us from doing wrong. Fathers and mothers don't do that to their children. And God wanted us to be his children, his family. He did not want to keep us in a zoo.

If everyone on earth became Christian, could we get rid of evil?

Ask yourself, "If everyone were as good a Christian as I am, would the world be a perfect place?" There will be evil in the world until Jesus returns to give us a new earth, simply because none of us can be perfect. This does not mean that we cannot improve our homes, our schools, our businesses, our governments, and our world. Every effort for good on our part will help. We have a right to look toward and work for a better future for our world.

Does that mean the world is both good and bad?

Yes, the world is both good and bad because we are both good and bad. We are good (and the world is good) because God made us (see Genesis 1:31). We are bad because we disobey God and separate ourselves from him (Ephesians 2:3). Both individually and together we act in ways that increase evil in the world. We can be restored to God and receive his power for goodness only by coming to him through Christ.

Are all people children of God?

In one sense, yes. In Ephesians 3:14-15 Paul says, "I bow my knees before the Father, from whom every family in heaven and on earth takes its name." But not all God's children have been gathered into the more intimate family of his church, into the body of Jesus Christ. Many of God's children live apart from him and do not worship him or bother to obey him. We who have been returned to God in Holy Baptism are now to be God's ambassadors to win these people back to God.

For reflection

1. Read Genesis 1:26-28 and Psalm 8 for insight into the high position and great responsibilities with which God honors us.

2. Reflect on what it means to be created by God. How does believing this change the way you live?

3. If God's creation is "good," why do so many bad things seem to happen?

2

A Word about God

More books have probably been written about God (and in earlier times, gods and goddesses) than about any other subject, even though the world has never seen a photograph of God, and no author has a tape recording of God's voice.

This book too is largely about God. In this chapter we shall only make a beginning, like an artist making the first, quick lines on a canvas before filling in the picture.

About two thousand years ago God (God the Son) lived on earth for thirty-three years as Jesus, a young man who grew up in the small town of Nazareth. Not everyone believes that Jesus was "God come into view." Christians do. This belief is the heart, the center, of everything we think or say about God. Without Jesus we would be mostly guessing about God.

But even apart from Jesus or without the Bible, we can learn some things about God simply by looking around. We do this often with people.

Let us say that I want to know you. I'm told I can find you in the garage, but you're not there. I look around. I see your motorcycle, sparkling clean. I see your tools, neatly arranged. I see photographs of mountains and flowers on the wall, pictures of places you've traveled. There are also pictures of a group of riders, your friends probably, arms around each other, laughing.

I say to myself, "He's a friendly person, orderly and neat, who loves beauty and the open road." Now I feel that I know something about you, but not enough. I want to know *you*.

So with God. God's universe is a vast precision machine, with stars and atoms moving in amazing order and with incredible speed and power. I see about me the colors of flowers and sunsets. I note the endless variety in birds, insects, snowflakes, and people. I say to myself, "God must be someone of tremendous power who loves order, variety, and beauty" (see Psalm 19:1).

What else can I say about God, until I have seen him? Nothing, really. From the stars and mountains I cannot really know whether he loves me or whether he simply passes me by.

If I am to know anything more, I must go to the Bible; I need to learn about Jesus.

From the Bible the most important thing you learn about God is that he loves you and that he is trying to reach you. He is pursuing you, running after you.

This, in fact, is how Christianity is different from every other religion in the world. All other religions picture people trying to reach God. Only in the Bible do you find the direction reversed. God is reaching out for people. The Bible tells us that on our own we cannot find God; we won't even try. Like Adam, we try to hide from God. Yet God keeps relentlessly pursuing us, hoping to catch up with us and bring us back home.

It is both comforting and disturbing to have a God like that. It is comforting because we don't have to rely on our own skills or goodness or intelligence to find him. It is disturbing too, because our lives may be drastically changed.

Maybe you think it would be nicer if he would sit in his heavenly office and wait for you to knock at the door, if and when you felt like it. Then you could go to him only when you are in trouble and need help.

But that's not the way it is. God is searching. God loves you, and you can't stop him from loving you and from running after you. You can try running away from God, but you cannot stop him from staying on your trail.

God is something like a good mother or father. Suppose their daughter is rebellious and thoughtless and runs away from home. Her parents will do everything they can to find her, because they love her. They want her back home, even if she remains rebellious and thoughtless. They hope she will become loving and thoughtful, but whether she changes or not, they want her because they love her.

God loves us like that. We are his children, and he wants us to be with him forever.

God wants above all to give you himself. God knows that you will not be truly happy until you have him. God will do many wonderful things for you—take away your loneliness, put you in touch with joy, and open your heart to love other people. God will honor you with big jobs to do, like managing the world and healing its hurts. But most of all, God simply wants you for himself.

If God loves me, how does he tell me about it?

In three basic ways: (1) God sends us sunshine and rain, oxygen to breathe, food to eat, color and sound to enjoy; (2) through the prophets and evangelists and apostles (the Bible), God gives us his Word; (3) God came in person to be with us in Jesus Christ, God the Son (Hebrews 1:1-2).

If I am inclined to run away from God, what does he use to stop me? Or does he just let me run?

In a very deep sense, God lets you run, but he catches up with you. Primarily, God uses the Word and the sacraments. If you stay out of reach of the Word and the Lord's Supper, if you never go to church and never read the Bible, God has a hard time catching up with you. He may use your experiences, like sickness or disappointments or failures, to reach you. He may also use some of your good friends. After all, God is an amazing strategist. But until the end, God will respect your right to either run away from him or run with him.

If I am really running away from God, why should I stop and let him reach me?

Simply because God is your Father. What happens after he reaches you is not as important as the fact that you and God are now together again.

It really would be a pity if the reason you wanted God was that you hoped he would do things for you—like making you happy. Maybe you tried other things—making money, collecting friends, taking trips—and they didn't make you happy. So, you decide to try God.

That's not a good enough reason for having God. Our Lord used another picture. "Listen! I am standing at the door, knocking," he said, and added that if anyone would open to him, he would come in (Revelation 3:20). Jesus made no promise of what gifts he would bring. He will enter—that should be reward enough. Of course he brings gifts, but the greatest gift is himself.

But Jesus does promise gifts, doesn't he?

He certainly does. The Bible is full of wonderful promises of the blessings he is ready to give his children. Christ summarized these in the simple words, "I came that they may have life, and have it abundantly" (John 10:10).

For reflection

1. Read Luke 15:11-32, the story of the prodigal son, and ask yourself if the son could have found happiness in the far country if he had prospered there, separated from his father.

2. Besides the image of God as a loving parent who is willing to forgive a rebellious child, what other image of God brings you comfort?

3. In what way does God most clearly express love for you?

3

One Book

The Christian church really has but one book. Of course thousands of books have been written about the faith, but all draw from the one book, the Bible. The Bible is the basis for our faith. It is of utmost importance to Christians.

We who are Christians believe that the Bible is different from all other books. It is not an encyclopedia where you can look up information about birds or stars. The whole world of chemistry and biology, for instance, is not in this book. God gives us this kind of knowledge largely through studies in science.

The Bible is God's book, and God reveals himself in it. God does not tell us everything about himself in this book, but he does tell us all that we need to know about him.

The strange thing about the Bible is that God uses it as a kind of door through which he comes to us. It is almost as if he leaps out of the pages to enter our hearts. Or think of the Bible as a lake. You sit on the bank fishing for knowledge about God. Suddenly God himself (not knowledge about him) takes the hook and pulls you in. God catches you.

By far the most important fact about the Bible is that Jesus Christ is in it. Luther said the Bible is like a cradle holding Jesus. If you were starting from scratch to read the Bible, you should probably first read the four Gospels, the accounts of Jesus' life and sayings. Something remarkable will then happen; you find that Jesus is more than the total of what he said and did. Jesus himself becomes the Word. You not only learn about God through him. You know God and are brought to him through Jesus.

When you read through all sixty-six books, and I hope you will, you will find some books more interesting and helpful than others. Some of them you will read over and over again, perhaps memorizing your favorite parts. You will feed on them for courage and hope and comfort. The 23rd Psalm and John 3:16 are probably memorized more often than any other parts of the Bible. But there are many, many more great passages.

The pity is that we don't read the Bible very much, even we who are Christians. Or when we do, we hurry through a few verses as if it is an unpleasant chore, like washing our hands before dinner—something Christians are expected to do.

The Bible can be exciting reading. Get a translation that appeals to you. Your pastor can help you choose one from the many versions now available. Try to be alone when you read. You can read through a Gospel in one sitting, in an hour or so. As you read, imagine that God is talking directly to you.

In what way is the Bible God's book? He didn't dictate the contents to the writers, did he?

No, certainly not. The books in the Bible were written by people, much like any other book, over the course of many centuries. But we believe that God had a hand in what was written. God "inspired" the writers (2 Peter 1:21). God also had a hand in assembling these particular books into one Bible, and has kept the book from being destroyed or lost these many centuries. God helps us to understand its great truths and even uses the book itself to give us the faith to receive it as his book.

Isn't the Bible a pretty old book to be of value in modern times?

It is an old book. The last parts of the Bible were written at least eighteen hundred years ago. If you're studying aeronautics, you certainly will not go to the Bible. But for knowledge about God, an old book may be better than a new one. Plato's Dialogues and Shakespeare's plays are old books too, but they remain the best of their kind in every university of the land. And the Bible—an old book, to be sure—is in a class by itself. It is the Word of God.

Are there mistakes or errors in the Bible?

The writers were mistaken, for instance, when they apparently indicated that the world was flat. We now know that the world is round. But God did not bother to bring the writers up to date in scientific matters. In his good time he gave this information to the astronomers and mathematicians. In some cases there also seem to be discrepancies or inconsistencies in the details of Bible stories. But these need not trouble us; they don't affect any Christian teaching. We believe that in all matters of faith and life the Bible is an infallible, sure guide. We can trust the Word, because it's the promises of God.

I have some trouble believing the miracles in the Bible. I don't think I have ever seen a miracle. Are these miracle stories like fairy tales?

No, miracle stories are real. And you may have seen more miracles than you know. You have never seen anyone walking on water, as Jesus did, but every day you see people flying like birds in airplanes. If people in Jesus' day had seen an airplane, they would surely have called it a miracle. Jesus healed the blind and deaf. Now, through medical knowledge that God has given to doctors, all sorts of people are healed. And because it happens every day, we take it for granted and forget to thank God for these really amazing miracles.

Is the Old Testament as important as the New Testament?

In one sense, yes. The Bible is a whole and has a story to tell, the story of God's love, from beginning to end. The climax of the story comes in the New Testament with the birth, life, death, and resurrection of Jesus. But the whole book is important. In a detective story, for instance, you would hardly say that the first chapter is less important than the last chapter, since the last chapter is very much tied up with the first. The Bible is something like that.

Would you advise that I read Genesis first, then Exodus—each of the sixty-six books in succession?

Not necessarily. In fact it may be best to begin in the New Testament with one of the Gospels. Then you will discover that all the other books, those before and those after, have a vital connection with the coming of Jesus.

Does God use the Bible to tell us what will happen in the future?

Yes, but God gives no calendar, nor does he describe the future in any detail. Throughout the Old Testament, for instance, he kept telling of the coming, someday, of the Messiah, Jesus Christ. In the New Testament he tells us that sometime Jesus will come again to usher in "a new heaven and a new earth," a new kind of life where pain and suffering and sin and death will be no more.

In almost every age people have tried to find in the Bible a time schedule or calendar for what may happen in the future, even setting a date for Christ's return, but no one has ever been successful. Jesus warned against doing this very thing (Mark 13:32-33). It is best to leave all this with God, and day by day to live as if Jesus were to return at any minute.

For reflection

1. Read 2 Timothy 3:14-17. Here the apostle Paul tells a young pastor, Timothy, what the Scriptures are for. Consider how the Bible helps you in each of the purposes listed here.

2. What part of the Bible speaks most directly to you? Why?

3. The Bible is sometimes described as "norm" for our faith and life. What does this mean to you?

4. What more would you like to know, or learn about, the Bible?

The Ten Commandments

4

The World of Rules

Anywhere you turn you run into rules, laws, or commandments. Some of them are made by God, some by people. All of God's rules are good, and most rules made by people are good.

Everything that God made in the universe is governed by God's rules that are sometimes called the laws of nature. And all of nature, from galaxies to insects, follows these laws automatically or instinctively. Human beings alone have the freedom to obey or disobey. They alone can rebel.

In the Garden of Eden God gave Adam and Eve a commandment which they disobeyed (Genesis 3:3, 6). This was the beginning of a long history of human disobedience and rebellion.

Much later, God gave the people of Israel the Ten Commandments. Moses was leading the people out of their bondage in Egypt. They were stranded in the desert, dissatisfied and rebellious. That is when God took Moses up into the mountain and gave him the Ten Commandments to govern his people. The Commandments contain the basic principles for those who want to know the will of God. In fact, they have become a guide for almost all the rules that people have made.

Think for a moment how much of your life is guided by rules. Your government has laws, places of business have regulations, and your home has rules. Schools, clubs, athletic teams—they all have rules. Our world is full of rules.

Most rules or laws are good. Some are not. Human history is one long struggle to get laws that are good and just. We do not always succeed. For many years there were laws that gave white people the right to buy and sell black people. In every country there is the danger of having the rich and powerful make laws unfair to the poor and powerless. Rules and laws made by human beings often fall short of the justice and mercy of God.

It is different with the Commandments of God. The Ten Commandments are all good and are given for our good. Some of them show us how to be good children of God. Some of them show us how to be good neighbors or friends of one another. The first three commandments center on God, the others on our relations with people.

If we obey them God has a chance to bless or reward us. If we break them, God, as a good Father, has no option but to punish us. He must try to stop us from doing those things which eventually would hurt us and others.

The fact is that none of us can obey the Commandments perfectly, no matter how hard we try. God knows this. God gave the Commandments to show us our desperate situation. Because of sin we stand before God's judgment, guilty and condemned. God knows that we will have to cry out for mercy and for forgiveness. And he has made provision for just that need.

Jesus Christ, the Son of God, became man, became our brother, and obeyed the will of God perfectly. He died on a cross for us to give us a right to be God's restored and pardoned children. We shall come to this wonderful truth later in our studies.

Is God angry when we disobey him?

Not in the same way that we may lose our tempers when someone steals or destroys something (see Psalm 103:8-9). But God is both hurt and angry. God is hurt when we ignore him and neglect to listen to his Word. He is angry when drugs and alcohol destroy people's lives. God is angry over wars that kill people and careless driving that injures people. God is angry over corruption in government and selfishness and greed in individuals. God cannot sit by and smile when we ignore his rules and hurt ourselves and others.

We certainly would not want a God who would sit by in good humor and dismiss all our wickedness and say, "Well, children will be children." We want a God of wrath, who is disturbed by evil.

How can you say that rules are good when it appears that they so often allow or support injustice?

To be without rules or laws altogether would leave us in utter confusion and chaos. Occasionally this has happened in a revolution. Everything falls apart. Looting and plundering and murder become rampant.

This does not mean that we defend bad laws or the miscarriage of justice. Jesus was crucified by the unjust application of law. Hitler murdered millions of Jews with a bad law. The United States allowed slavery through a bad law, and mistreated Indians with bad laws. Other countries have done the same.

The answer is not to get rid of rules and laws, but to get good ones. We have many fine leaders in all levels of government working hard to provide good laws and to make just application of law.

If a law is bad, should you break it?

At times, if the law is really harmful. The Bible says that we must obey God rather than human authority (Acts 5:29). But few laws are that bad. They may only be unwise or inadequate, and then we should obey them. At the same time, we should not take advantage of laws that permit acts that are not in accord with God's will.

If you do break a law of the land, you must be prepared to pay the penalty. Martin Luther King, the great black leader who was assassinated, openly broke several laws he regarded wrong in God's sight, but he was ready to pay the penalty. He went to jail; he paid fines. He did this to call attention to those laws which he believed to be wrong.

The Ten Commandments were given thousands of years ago. Do they really fit now?

Yes, indeed. Test them. Take them, one by one, and ask yourself which you would eliminate. These are God's rules, after all, and God does not make mistakes. Some words need to be brought up to date. The Commandments speak about coveting oxen. For most of us it would be more pertinent to talk about stealing cars or jewelry or money. But the meaning is the same. Moreover, the summary of all the Commandments remains the same: love God and your neighbor.

Has anyone ever succeeded in keeping all God's Commandments?

No one (Romans 3:10). If God were to accept us only when we had obeyed all his rules perfectly, none of us would make it. He would have an empty heaven, except for angels. God accepts us as his children because Jesus, who did obey all God's laws perfectly, died for us. God credits us through faith with the perfect obedience of Jesus, and thus looks on us as if we were perfect. We thank Jesus for making us right with God.

If Jesus has obeyed all the Commandments for us, why should we worry about them?

If we want to find ways to thank God for what he has done for us, we shall try to obey the Commandments. We obey them to please our Lord, not to win credits that will make us acceptable to God. Jesus has won all the credits for us. To love these great and good Commandments and try to obey them is our way of making our Lord glad.

For reflection

1. Read Exodus 19-20 for the background of the Ten Commandments and to get an understanding of how important it was for these disordered desert people to have rules.

2. For what purposes has God given us rules, commandments?

3. Why ought we obey God's commands?

5

What Other Gods?

I am the Lord your God.
You shall have no other gods.

There is but one God. The Bible presents him in three persons: God the Father, God the Son, and God the Holy Spirit. But God is one.

In earlier times people actually did shape other gods from stone or wood or precious metals (Isaiah 40:19-20). That's almost unheard of today.

At other times emperors or kings have claimed to be divine and demanded that people not only obey them but also bow down and worship them (Daniel 3).

Almost every civilization has its legends of gods and goddesses. Greece had its Zeus, Apollo, Artemis, and others. If you travel to Athens today you may see the remarkable Parthenon, which was erected in honor of these gods.

The ancient Roman gods were Jupiter, Mars, Minerva, and others. In the North European countries, names of the gods were Woden or Odin, Thor, Balder, plus a company called the Valkyries. There is a rich legendary literature about the gods and goddesses of these several civilizations.

It is notable that in all this profusion of gods and goddesses, only in the little country of Israel was there a clear call to worship one God and him alone. This, we believe, was because God had chosen to reveal himself especially to this nation, and then from this nation to the world.

We no longer have idols or worship kings, but we still have other gods. We still tend to exalt things, people, and goals to a position equal to or above the true God. The First Commandment "You shall have no other gods before me" is addressed as much to us as to ancient peoples.

Let us examine some of these rivals to the worship of God.

First, *success*. We live in a success-oriented society. Everyone wants to be a winner. And we measure success by what people around us call success. A student who gets good marks is a success; the teacher says so. A person with a good job and a good salary is a success; the boss says so. A rich person is a success; people powerful enough to get their own way are successes, because the world regards them so.

We turn to someone other than God to determine what success is and what we ought to do to win it. We make the world the judge, and not God. This is not at all what God wants. We are in fact worshiping at the wrong altar, fearing and trusting and loving something or someone other than God.

A second rival is *praise*, which is the twin of success. We become hungry for the praise of people. We want approval and popularity. We are disturbed when someone criticizes us. We live in fear that people may discover our weaknesses and call us failures.

Yet the strange thing is that the more successful we are and the more people praise us, the more filled with anxiety we become. What if people should stop praising us? What if we can't measure up to their expectations?

Pleasure is a third rival. The Lord wants us to enjoy his world. But if we are in an endless chase to find new sources of pleasure—a new car, a new home, a new outfit, new friends, a new spouse, a new vacation spot—then the search for pleasure becomes a god.

A fourth rival is *security*. God wants us to have food and shelter and health. Jesus even asks us to pray for these needs: "Give us this day our daily bread." The moment we put these in first place, however, we are on a path that has no end. We spend our time, energies, and worries on being safe. We can't give as God wants us to give because we are afraid we may need our money. We can't risk helping someone because we might have to keep on helping. Besides, we aren't well; the doctor has told us to be careful. We fear, love, and trust the god of security, and we become dull and selfish.

These modern deities take many forms. They threaten to become our idols, and to elbow God out of our hearts.

Since almost every civilization worships something, doesn't this prove that there must be a God?

Not really. You cannot prove the existence of God as you would prove the existence of a plant or of a mathematical proposition. God is not found with a microscope or telescope. You *know* that two plus two equals four. You *believe* in God. God has given us the kind of mind that can both know and believe. Knowledge is neither more sure nor higher than belief. Both are gifts of God.

Does it matter much what kind of God we believe in, as long as we are religious and sincere?

Very much. There is but one true God. Moreover, the kind of God we worship determines finally what kind of lives we live. We worship God, the Father of our Lord Jesus Christ and *our* Father, the God revealed in the Bible. This is vastly different from worshiping the god of Islam of Hinduism or a modern cult (see Luke 4:8).

Some say that money and power are the chief objects of our idolatry. Is this true?

Money and power easily become idols. People may initially want money so they can educate their children and help people in need. But often money becomes an end in itself and becomes more important than either children or needy people. A person may want power to be able to do good things for the country and for people, but again, power itself can become the god.

We praise work as a good thing. Can work be an idol?

Yes, it is possible. I once knew a man who had worked hard since he was a boy. He owned much land and money; he was rich. He had a heart attack at fifty-two. I told him, "John, take it easy. You don't have to work anymore." He replied rather sadly, "All my life I have learned to do but one thing—work. Now I'm too old to learn anything else." A year later, working again, he dropped dead one day near his truck. He was a good man, a God-fearing man, but he really had made an idol of work. Many people do. It is said of us in our country that we don't know how to do anything but work. Even when we play, we make hard work of it.

Can you make an idol of something you don't have?

Yes, the desire for something can itself be an idol. You may want something so much that you dream about it night and day. You may want something so much that you become miserable thinking about it. Sometimes these desires turn into misplaced actions. A young man desires a car so much that he steals it. A young women may want something so much that she tucks it in her handbag without paying for it. Desires can become gods.

How can you avoid making such things gods?

Put them in their right place. Most of these things, in their right place, may be good. Place God in the highest place, and then ask God for help to arrange things according to importance.

For reflection

1. Read Mark 10:17-22 and think about why an otherwise fine man became guilty of idolatry.

2. How do you honor God above all other things?

3. What is most challenging about putting God first in your life?

6

A Name to Honor

You shall not take the name of the Lord your God in vain.

Why do people swear and curse using the name of God? Do you think God cares? Or does God sit in heaven and chuckle about it? In this commandment he warns us not to use his name in vain, or carelessly. In fact, it is the only commandment of the ten where he threatens specifically to punish if we disobey.

A person's name is not just another word. In a deep sense, your name is you. The way people use your name shows how they feel about you. If people love you, they will speak your name with tenderness. If they fear you, they will say your name with respect. If they adore you, they will speak your name with a kind of reverence. If on the other hand they hate you or despise you, they will probably talk about you sneeringly, with scorn and contempt.

God's name represents all that God has revealed about himself.

When people throw God's name around carelessly or are indifferent about his will, they show that they don't think much of God. They may not intend to despise God, but they certainly do not show that they fear or love or honor him. Rather, they show that they do not take God seriously. They really reduce God to nothing. Such persons indicate that God is not worth fearing, loving, or trusting.

Apparently there is something deep within us that wants to get rid of God. We don't want to be under his control. Nor do we really want his help. We want to go it alone. So we toss God's name into the garbage heap. We use it as if he means nothing to us.

We would show God more respect if we never used his name at all, whether in church or on the streets. In the early period of Israel, people stood in such awe of God that they never spoke his name, even in praise of him. They did not feel worthy to have this wonderful, holy name cross their lips. They honored God by never saying his name.

But we have been invited to speak it. Jesus told us to address God with boldness and trust, to say, "Our Father who art in heaven." He urged us to call on the name of God in prayer. He told us to praise and thank him. Because Jesus died on a cross for us, he opened the door of the Father's house to us and gave us a right to be children of God (see Hebrews 4:16).

Is swearing or cursing as bad as stealing or killing?

You won't go to jail for cursing, as you will for stealing or killing. But if using God's name in vain is the same as getting rid of God, then this is the worst thing that can happen to you or to the world. You get rid of a person by killing him. You can't kill God, but you can kill his name by tossing it away, which is what you do when you use his name without prayer, praise, and thanksgiving (see Deuteronomy 5:11).

Why do so many respectable people swear or curse?

Probably for two reasons. First, each of us has a secret desire not to take God too seriously, to keep him at a distance, or to be rid of him altogether. We are proud to cope with life on our own. So instead of calling on God to save us and guide us, we toss his name to the winds. The second reason is that we simply fall into the habit of swearing and cursing.

If it's only a habit, is it so bad?

If you had a habit of stealing bicycles or killing people, you certainly would not say, "It's only a habit; I really don't mean it." A bad habit is bad, the damage we do out of habit is bad, and to be controlled by a bad habit is bad.

If I saw someone trying to steal my friend's bicycle, I'd try to stop him. Should I try to stop people from swearing?

Yes, but you will need to do it at the right time and in the right way. If a person says "By God" or "Damn it," it may not be wise to stop him while he is talking and correct him on the spot. It is wiser, and more kind, to find a chance to talk to him about it later. Just to denounce cursing is not enough. Help the person to see that his attitude toward God is unhealthy.

If I am to make any impression—in the world of business, for instance—won't I have to swear as others do?

You may think so, but that's really a very phony excuse. If you're selling a car, for instance, no one is going to buy because you say "This is a damn good car" instead of "This is a top-notch car." In our language, as in our lives, we need not conform to the world or say and do what everyone else says and does (Romans 12:2).

How can I best break the habit of swearing and cursing?

The best way is to increase your use of God's name in the right way. You drive out a bad habit by forming a good habit. You pray. You praise God. You thank God. You keep thinking of everything God does for you. God gives you life, forgives your sins, and promises to love you forever. Keep thinking how wonderful God is, and soon you actually may not be able to use his name except in a good way.

Is an interest in the occult, astrology, palmistry, and such things a way of honoring God's name?

Hardly. God warns against such practices. People who have these interests are usually trying to find ways to deal with problems without God. Most likely they are calling for something other than the forgiveness of sins or a life in fellowship with God. But if they are not just doing it as a game, they may be indicating that they have given up on their proud self-confidence and are reaching out for some sort of help from "the other world." Their reaching out may make them willing to hear about God.

For reflection

1. Read Exodus 3:13-15. What conclusions can you draw from the answer that God gave when Moses asked for his name?

2. Cursing by using the name of God or Jesus has become extremely common. How can Christians change this trend?

3. How will you honor God's holy name in your life?

7

One Day a Week

Remember the Sabbath day, to keep it holy.

A club such as the Rotary Club has had a rule that any member who misses a meeting must make it up by attending the meeting of another club, even if he has to go to another town. Members must attend the meetings, or they're out.

The church has no such rule. You can miss the church service and still be a member, though your absence may be harmful to you.

God has one great and inclusive command: love God and love one another. All the rest of God's rules are in support of that first one, guideposts on the path of love. That's what this Third Commandment is too. It's hardly likely that the Lord checks attendance every Sunday morning. (Yet I suspect God knows who's there and who isn't, since his eye is even on the sparrow.)

It would seem strange, however, if a person who loves God and wants to honor his name did not show up in the place and at the time set aside specifically to listen to God and to thank him. What would you think of a football player who didn't bother to attend scheduled practice sessions? People would conclude that he didn't care much whether he continued to be a member of the team or not.

I knew a man who had not missed Sunday services in 31 years, except the one time he was sick. He didn't earn extra credits with God, of course, because Jesus Christ had won for him all the credits necessary. He pleased God by worshiping, to be sure. But more important, he gave God a chance, through Word and sacrament, to give him strength and comfort and hope. And of course by simply being present he encouraged everyone else who was there.

Oliver Wendell Holmes, one of America's great supreme court judges, was always in church on Sundays. He said that he had a little plant in his heart that needed watering at least once a week.

It is estimated that only about 40 percent of America's church membership is in church on any given Sunday. That's not a great record. Even so, you can add up all the fans that attend all the athletic games in the country—professional, amateur, university, high school; the whole crowd in any given year—and they will be but a small percentage of the people who find their way to the churches and synagogues of the land.

It's a pity, however, that it's not 80 percent or 90 percent who attend church. Most western governments today encourage citizens to belong to a church, to attend it, and to support it. In the early church, during the first century, the followers of Jesus came together for worship at the risk of their lives. They gathered in secret, in the catacombs of Rome for instance, to hear God's word and to pray to him. There are still countries where you are likely to be discriminated against if you go to church.

In the pioneer days, people worked in factories or on farms ten to fourteen hours a day, six days a week. Sunday became for them both a day of rest and a day for church worship. Often they had to walk many miles to church, or ride in buggies or wagons.

In a day when most of us can reach our beautiful churches with no danger of persecution and with little inconvenience, it must sadden God to have us absent when he is there ready to give us his rich gifts.

I find it difficult to see the importance of setting aside a specific day for worship.

All the days of the week are God's days, but to set aside one special day for the corporate worship of God is of strategic importance. That day does not have to be Saturday (as for the Jews) or Sunday (as chosen by Christians), but the principle of the Lord's day is important.

In the days of Hitler's Germany, Hitler set out to weaken the church. He did this by robbing the church of the Lord's day. He demanded that all the young people of Germany meet for marches on Sunday. It was said that Hitler did not need to kill the preachers to destroy the church. All he needed to do was to steal the Lord's day from the church. With no Hitler to tyrannize us, we can largely kill the church by sheer default, by not exercising the privilege and discipline of using the day to worship God (see Hebrews 10:24-25).

What is there about the church service that's so important?

Chiefly the Word and the sacraments. God has decided to come to us through his Word and sacraments, as means of grace. Through his Word he addresses you. With his body and blood he feeds you. Instead of judging a sermon on the basis of whether it can arouse your interest, try listening to see if God has something to say to you through it. You may be surprised. In an otherwise rather ordinary sermon, even a dull one, God may break through with some message especially for you. He does come to us through his Word (see Matthew 18:20).

Will I be changed by going to church?

You will be changed probably without noticing it. God's Word will find its way into your heart, whether you are aware of it or not. You will be strengthened and comforted. Even if you can't point to any single moment of unusual excitement, there will be a gradual buildup within you, which in time, you will find of value. It's almost like putting a few dollars in a savings account, week after week, and after a while realizing that you have hundreds of dollars. The Word of God is like that.

Every Sunday we seem to do the same things in our service, don't we?

Yes, it may be the same service. In fact it is most likely the same service the people of God have used for centuries. It's exhilarating to think that by these same words our grandparents and ancestors for generations have come into the presence of God—sometimes the exact words, perhaps the same hymns. For hundreds of years millions of believers have prayed to God in the words of the Lord's Prayer and have confessed their faith in the words of the Apostles'

Creed. When you use these old words, imagine that you are joined by the hundreds of millions who both now and in ages past have come to God with these words.

Every congregation will use other forms too in some of its services, and that's good. But let's not overlook the power and beauty of saying and hearing the words that are as old as the church itself.

For reflection

1. Read Mark 2:23-27; 3:1-6; and 6:1-6 to learn about Jesus' attitude toward the Sabbath observance of his day. Imagine what he might say about our Sunday observance.

2. Why is it important to set aside time for worshiping God? What happens to us when we don't?

3. What part of worship "speaks" to you?

8

Loaned to Love

Honor your father and your mother.

The most important family you have is the big family of God, the Christian church. At baptism you were brought into this family. Your church family circles the whole world, and it even includes those who have left this world and now live in heaven.

The family next in importance is your own—parents and children, brothers and sisters. God loans us to each other to love one another.

You did not choose your parents, nor your brothers and sisters. In a sense, they did not choose you either, even though they wanted you. Before you were born or before you were adopted, they didn't know precisely what sort of person you would be. Now we are thrown together, and we all have the privilege and the task of wanting each other and loving each other.

If you are a son or daughter, remember it might have been easier for your parents if they did not have you—or any children. Without children they would be free to come and go whenever they chose, and they would have more money to spend. They would not have to worry about you when you are sick. But they want you.

If you are a parent remember that, more than anyone else, you will determine the outcome of your child's life. If making money and having fine things are your important concerns, these are the values your children will have. If you are indifferent about church, it will be difficult for them to take God and his will seriously. If success (however that's defined) is more important to you than honesty and compassion for others, you'll probably have children who will use people for their own purposes instead of being true friends. By what you say and do, you are your children's prime teachers.

We have much power over each other in the family. Children have frightening power. They more than anyone else can make their parents glad or sad. Parents have awesome power. By their love and wise counsel they can encourage love for God and become God's agents, giving their children a sense of worth and security, compassion for others, and courage for the future.

Surrounding your family are others (sometimes called your extended family) who also love you and try to help you. They are uncles and aunts, grandparents, cousins, teachers, pastors, friends, neighbors. They are aided by others in positions of responsibility in schools, government, and society. Thank God for all the reinforcement these people give you. Cherish their friendship, and give them yours.

No person, and no family, is sufficient unto itself. And if a family turns in upon itself, even if it achieves love among its members, it becomes selfish, indulgent, and spiritually impoverished. For its own health, it needs to get outside itself in fellowship with other families.

The home is the basic laboratory for life. There we can learn to live with each other in patience and forgiveness. There we learn obedience and respect for authority. There, embraced by love, we can get a clue to the love of our great heavenly Parent. In every society throughout history, the family has been the foundation institution. As the family goes, so go the country and the world.

Why does God tell children to honor their parents? Why doesn't God also tell parents to honor their children?

He does, over and over again, in many parts of the Bible (Ephesians 6:4; Deuteronomy 6:6-7). God's commands to parents are exacting and his expectations of them very high. To be parents is the highest office women and men can have. But this particular commandment, the fourth, is addressed to sons and daughters.

What threats to the family need we guard against?

There are all sorts. Obviously each member has to be alert against preoccupations that make him or her forget to be cheerful, charitable, and cooperative. But there are forces in the very way we live that may spin us apart. Activities and responsibilities in school, work, or elsewhere, may rob the family of time together. It takes careful engineering for families to have time together. At whatever cost, families should find ways. The stakes are high, both for character and for happiness.

If my parents fail me, can I still honor them?

It may be difficult, but we can still honor their position. If you can't be proud of your parents, you can try to understand their failings and maybe help them. If a father drifts into alcoholism, loses his job, and even goes to jail, you can try to understand how this could happen. Did he have fears, maybe for you, and worries that you never knew? Your understanding, your forgiveness, and your love may be the very thing he needs to make a new start.

Can I honor my parents if they leave each other?

Separation or divorce is failure, and you can hardly honor them for failure. But each of us fails at some time, and despite their divorce, there are still many reasons why you should honor your parents. You may feel that they did not love you enough to stay together for your sake. They may feel very badly about this too and still love you, in spite of the weakness, stubbornness, and wretchedness that may have driven them apart. Each of them, now separated from the other, may need your love and forgiveness more than ever.

Shouldn't parents praise their children more than they do?

Most parents are much more proud of their children than the children will ever know. When someone tells them, "What a fine daughter and son you have," their spirits soar with joy. They may even boast of their children's achievements to others, but rarely say much to their children. Perhaps they should express their pride more, but failure to do so may only mean that they are not surprised that their children do well. They have learned to expect good things from them.

I wish my folks would stop worrying about me. I don't think they trust me.

They may not trust your judgment all the time. In their concern for you they may not seem to trust you. They lie awake if you're not yet at home. Why don't they just go to sleep? Remember that fifty thousand people are killed on U. S. highways each year, and the majority are young people. The morning paper might carry your name. Wouldn't you be disappointed if they did not have some fears, even if these fears seem to indicate that they don't trust you?

For reflection

1. Read Luke 2:41-51. What can you conclude about the family life of Jesus? About his extended family?

2. What is the most important ingredient in making a family strong?

3. What is the biggest threat to unity in the family?

4. How is the church like family?

9

Reverence for Life

You shall not kill.

Dr. Albert Schweitzer in many ways is the most celebrated example in our century of a life given to others. Already in his early 30s, he was a distinguished theologian and philosopher and the most acclaimed organist in Europe. Suddenly he puzzled everyone by turning to medicine and going to the interior of Africa to spend his life healing people there.

The term *reverence for life* describes Schweitzer's attitude. He went to such extremes that he would not knowingly kill any living thing, not even the ants that busied themselves on his table.

Reverence for human life is etched deeply in all humanitarian circles, certainly in the Christian faith. We take seriously that God is the Giver of all life. We also believe that death is not one of God's gifts, but in biblical language an enemy, "the last enemy" which God has set out to oppose and at least to overcome, once and for all. If we take seriously God's command "Thou shalt not kill," we are arrayed with God in opposing anything that destroys human life. And as a consequence of Christ's resurrection from the dead, we are confident that life, not death, will have the last word.

For these reasons questions concerning war, capital punishment, abortion, and euthanasia become perplexing. Do we ever, under any circumstances, have a right to destroy or end life? Must we not do everything we can to preserve life? Are there values even greater than life itself that warrant either destroying it or giving it up?

Perhaps we must first define what we mean by *life*. Is life simply a state in which a person breathes and the heart beats? Or is it more properly the state in which the brain is functioning and a person is consciously capable of reasoning, knowing others, loving, and

enjoying things? If the brain is gone, is life still there? Modern medicine is able to keep a heart beating long after the brain is dead. Is
such a person dead or alive? Our society faces some difficult issues
with this commandment.

The commandment of course means that you are not to take a
gun and shoot someone. We understand that. Unfortunately, it is
sometimes necessary for governments to use force to protect people
from those who would take their lives.

We also can see that it is our duty to heal the sick, to feed the
hungry, to prevent accidents—to exert every effort to sustain life. It
would seem that this commandment also implies that it is our duty
to help one another have the kind of life that we term "the good
life"—with friendship and love and enjoyment.

There is a still deeper level of life to consider for those of us who
are Christian. We believe that in addition to physical life, there is a
life with God, eternal life, the life of the soul, the life that is restored
after death so we can live with God forever. To have this life people
need more than food and oxygen, or even intelligence and friends.
We need the gospel, the Word of God, sometimes called "the bread
of life." Jesus called himself that bread, as well as the water of life.
He said that if anyone causes another to lose that life, it would have
been better if that person had not been born.

But Jesus was also deeply concerned about physical life. He
healed the sick and fed the hungry, and told his followers to do the
same (see Matthew 25:40). The history of the Christian church is a
glorious story of his followers reaching out to sustain life. No institution in the world, and no other religion in the world, has such a
noble record of building hospitals, caring for the poor and neglected,
and in general being sensitive to the sufferings of people.

Reverence for life will be taken seriously only if we believe
that people are more than organisms that breathe and think. If we
are no more than high-grade mammals, complex animals that
write oratorios and invent computers, but animals still, cousins of
the rat and the chimpanzee, then we shall tend to treat each other
as animals.

But we believe people are children of God and that their bodies are dwelling places for God himself. This makes all the difference in the world. The commandment then becomes, "Thou shalt not kill sons and daughters of the eternal King."

Isn't war the most flagrant disobedience of this commandment?

Yes, in a very real sense. In earlier societies of course it was often a choice between killing and being killed. We used to speak of just wars, and wars that were clearly wars of self-defense against an aggressor. Now, with nations so interdependent and with the massive instruments of destruction we have, it is increasingly difficult to think of war as ever being justified. In fact, peace among nations and outlawing war are now the world's most critical issues, more critical than hunger or overpopulation. A big atomic war could be suicide for the world.

Is war always wrong, then?

To destroy life is wrong. But to take away a people's freedom— their property and their duty and opportunity to care for one another—is also wrong. When these values are threatened by an oppressor, people out of good conscience have chosen to defend them, even at the cost of killing the enemy. Others, from equally good conscience, have chosen not to defend these values by war, and the government has exempted them as "conscientious objectors."

With the threat of overpopulation, shouldn't we prevent life's coming into being?

There are worldwide programs of birth control, one or another of which is generally accepted by major religious groups. The argument is that if there is food supply for a limited number, to bring additional life into the world is to starve (in a sense, kill) others. The possibilities are no doubt real, and great care in planning must be taken.

Is the control of birth the same as abortion?

No, abortion is cutting off or ending life that already is. If a fetus or embryo is likely to cause the death of its mother, the question will be whether to try to save the child or the mother. Usually the decision is for the mother.

Is suicide the same as killing someone else?

Not quite. God gives us no more right to destroy ourselves than to destroy someone else. Most suicides are by people who, for the moment, are so depressed about themselves and the future that they give up. They often have become so confused that they are hardly responsible for their act.

I hear people talk about the right to die. What does that mean?

Some people maintain that a person in full possession of his or her reason has a right to choose the time of his or her death. If, for instance, a woman has incurable cancer and faces long suffering and medical bills that will impoverish her family, should she have the right to request or order her own death? Or, if a man is old and faces a long and lingering decline of his faculties, including ability to remember or talk, so that he will become a burden to society and his family, should he have a right to die before that happens? If such people decide to take their own lives, this would seem to be a form of suicide.

This commandment, the fifth, does indeed confront us with issues that will tax both the wisdom and the conscience of our day and the future.

For reflection

1. Read Joel 3:1-4. Examine the vision of the prophet and ask what we might do to work toward his vision.

2. Do you believe there are circumstances that warrant—even call for—killing another human being?

3. What contributes to violence in our society? How can we "turn down" the violence?

10

Where Sex Belongs

You shall not commit adultery.

We live our lives within many different circles. Within each we have relationships with other people. Some circles are large, some small.

Our school or the place we work is one circle. Within it are some people who like us, and we like them. Our home is a circle, and there we know a special kind of love and special kinds of relationships—parents, children, brothers, sisters. Our church is a circle where we share a faith with others. Some we know well, some hardly at all.

The smallest circle is marriage. Two people who "fall in love" promise to remain a circle of just two persons for life. They give themselves to each other in fullness and completeness that no other circle demands. This is the deepest and most intimate relationship of all. And it is into this circle that God has placed the gift of sexual life.

Friendship is different. This too is a wonderful circle. You may like a great number of people and call them friends, but most people have a relatively small circle of special friends. From the time we are children we tend to gravitate to a few who are especially close to us. A little girl will bring a classmate home and say to her mother, "Mom, this is my friend." She separates her out from her other playmates.

We do this to the end of life. Two people are drawn together, like David and Jonathan in the Bible, not biologically, not out of common tastes in politics or even religion, not out of equality in wealth or intelligence. Somehow they find each other a warmth, an openness, an understanding, and a trust. They demand nothing of each other; they simply enjoy one another. This is not the same as "falling in love."

If friends were to have sexual relations with each other, their friendship would be so changed that it would be gone—simply because God does not intend sexual acts to be a part of friendship. In fact, such use—or misuse—of sex will destroy friendship. A new relationship emerges which can only grow more distasteful as the friends realize their friendship is gone.

And certainly sex never belongs between chance acquaintances, or between people who simply like each other, even though the act may give momentary pleasure. Sex is never a detached pleasure, like eating a good meal. That you can do alone. You use food to satisfy a hunger. In sexual relations outside of marriage you *use* another person as an object to satisfy lust.

Only in marriage, where two people love one another, need one another, and have made a lifelong commitment to each other—only in that God-ordered circle can sex be trusted not to be a need apart, like food, but something that becomes at once a beautiful act of giving and needing.

Most of the books and articles written about sex give instructions on how to get the most pleasure from the act, as if it is of no importance who the persons may be. People are treated as sexual animals, each using the other (whether a stranger or not) for his or her satisfaction. These publications are virtually manuals on mechanical engineering and miss what is significant about sex. Countless people, both young and old, are lured into lives of sin, unhappiness, anxiety, and often lifelong regrets—by separating sex from marriage.

God will not be mocked. We cannot outsmart him. He has made us, after all. He, better than we, knows where this delicate, glorious, and mysterious gift belongs. And he has said clearly that it belongs in the circle of marriage. His command is explicit against fornication (the sexual act between unmarried persons) and against adultery (the act between a married person and another, not the spouse) see Galatians 5:19-21.

Sexual activity is not necessary for a full life. Even in marriage it is but one of the gifts (certainly not the most enduring) which gives splendor to the joys of husbands and wives. And countless people have known immeasurably rich relationships in the other circles that God provides.

If a person doesn't marry or have a sex partner, is he or she abnormal?

Of course not. Sex is not the whole of life, and a person may choose to live a lifetime in the other circles with fullness and happiness. Our society is warped at this point. Even beautiful friendships are under suspicion by our age that has blown sex out of proportion. Many people think it unnatural and even unworthy that whole groups, like priests and nuns, renounce marriage in order to give greater service to God and the church.

If two people really love each other, need they marry to have sexual relations?

God says yes. If they feel deep love for each other, in marriage they reinforce their feelings by a public promise. Feelings of love may at times be strong, at times weak. If feelings are buttressed by the promise that, come what may, they will be faithful to each other and care for each other for life, then the relationship can be strong enough to entrust to it the precious gift of sex.

If a marriage fails, is the reason always adultery?

No, there may be many other reasons. None of them need be serious enough to end the marriage if the wife and husband have the strength and patience to work at overcoming whatever separates them. Even adultery need not end the marriage if they meet one another with repentance and forgiveness (see Matthew 19:3-9).

How can people best guard against divorce?

Most important of all, by taking great care in preparing for marriage. It is also important to bring to it a life that is basically unselfish. In marriage, remember that you have God's lavish forgiveness for the past and his great readiness to help you over the hurdles that come.

How should one prepare for marriage?

You start early. The habits you form in your relations with other people—your parents and brothers and sisters and friends—will carry over into your marriage. If you are self-centered, unloving to other people, rarely thanking anyone, usually blaming other people for your troubles, you may be a risk for marriage. You don't change the moment you stand at the altar and make promises. Putting Christ first in your life helps you to be more loving to others.

How much alike should two people be who get married?

You need not be alike to have a good marriage. There must be love, of course. You must be deeply attracted to each other. It is helpful if your differences are not too great. To be of similar cultural and educational backgrounds, while not guaranteeing a good marriage, may eliminate some potential trouble spots. It is very important to share the same general set of values and to have a common faith. To worship together regularly at your church is to give the Lord a chance to keep strengthening your marriage.

For reflection

1. Read Hosea 1-3, where God's forgiveness and restoration of his people is likened to a husband's forgiveness of an adulterous wife.

2. How would you describe our society's attitude toward sex and sexuality?

3. How should our faith affect our attitude and actions?

4. Describe an ideal friendship and an ideal marriage.

11

On Honesty

You shall not steal.
You shall not bear false witness against your neighbor.

If a person does not steal or lie, we call that person honest. Let us imagine such a person, and call her Jane. Let's have her be a teacher.

As a girl Jane was told that stealing and lying were both wrong and stupid. Her parents told her, her Sunday school teachers told her, in fact, almost everyone told her. Once, when she had cheated in an examination, she realized that she had really stolen. She had stolen information (from a book under her desk), and had lied to her teacher, giving him the impression that she knew the answer. She didn't enjoy the good grade she got, and decided this wouldn't happen again.

Later, in high school, she and her friend Molly each told their folks that they would be staying overnight with the other (Molly with Jane, and Jane with Molly) to study. Instead they went with some dates to the next town, and both stayed at Mary's house; Mary's parents were away. Jane's parents trusted her, and a couple days later Jane decided she'd have to tell her folks. She couldn't stand living with a lie.

At the university she lived in a small dormitory with twenty other girls. One day, bursting into a friend's room to get a book, she surprised another girl, Sally, emptying out her friend's purse. The girls had been missing some money before and already suspected Sally. Instead of telling her friend or the housemother, Jane took Sally into her room and convinced her that she should confess her thefts and return all the money she had stolen. They became good friends, and Sally was forever thankful to Jane.

Now Jane had become a teacher. It bothered her to no end when she overheard some girls talking about their shoplifting, or when a boy lied about a book he had borrowed from the library and lost, or when she heard about someone stealing from another's locker. It bothered her, too, when students would say unkind things about others behind their backs.

It wasn't only her students who troubled Jane. When she heard other teachers talking about how they did not report all their earnings to the government for income tax purposes, or how they claimed incorrect exemptions, she wondered how they could be trusted in other things.

And when she read the newspaper about people in business who deceived their customers, or learned of professions that charged unreasonable fees, or heard about government leaders who accepted bribes, she was discouraged.

But when she was tempted to think these pessimistic thoughts, she pulled herself up short and said to herself, "What am I doing? I'm forgetting all my friends who are honest. I'm forgetting the splendid leaders in government who do have integrity. I'm forgetting the great numbers of people in business and the professions who are trustworthy. I can't let myself lose faith in people because there is some dishonesty in the world."

We are all tempted at one time or another to be less than honest. We need to remember that to be known as a trustworthy person is one of the finest tributes that can be given us.

Most people try to be honest, don't they?

Yes. Just think of the people you know best. Would they lie to you or steal from you? While we cannot be blind to the dishonesty that does exist in the world, why not conclude that most of the people you don't know personally are honest too?

I like the account of the farmer in pioneer days who bought a cow for $100 on the assurance that she would yield twenty quarts of milk a day. When he got the cow, he discovered that she gave twenty-five quarts. So, instead of chuckling over the good deal he had made, he went back and paid another $20 for her. He didn't have to, of course. The deal had been made. But he was an honest man (excessively honest, you might think). He thought this was the fair thing to do.

It would be a sorry world if people were honest only because they feared the consequences of dishonesty, wouldn't it?

If that were the case the whole fabric of our kind of government and society would be in deep trouble. We would eventually need a vast law enforcement staff, a whole army of auditors checking everyone's income tax returns. Ultimately we would become a police state where everyone is assumed to be guilty until he proves that he is innocent. A good government never rests on laws and police, but on the integrity and honesty of its people.

Should I speak well of a person when I know it's not true?

No, you can't lie just to be kind. If you are asked to recommend someone for a job, for instance, to be fair to the prospective employer you must stick to the facts. But you also should call attention to all the good qualities the person may have.

It is a good rule never to speak ill of a person unless it is necessary to do so. And in judging people we ought to give them the benefit of the doubt and put the best construction on what they say and do (see Matthew 7:1-5).

I think it's a good idea to trust people, but isn't it a bit naïve to trust everybody?

Yes, you must recognize the temptation most people have of stretching the truth. But basically it's a bad idea to walk around being suspicious of everything and everybody. You'd probably be going a bit too far not to discount some of the claims made in advertising, for example.

In summary, what do these Seventh and Eighth Commandments tell us?

Be honest, even to a fault. Never take unfair advantage of anyone's property or interests, but help people keep and care for what is theirs. Never lie to anyone, or about anyone. Trust people. It's better to trust too much than too little. Speak well of people. If you can't say anything good, keep still.

For reflection

1. Read Acts 5:1-11 and think of how the case of Ananias and Saphhira relates to the Seventh and Eighth Commandments.

2. What is your reaction to the idea that we have become more selfish or self-centered as a society?

3. What problems result from wanting more or getting joy or power from purchasing or owning possessions?

12

Your Right to Wish

You shall not covet.

You get ready to blow out the candles on your birthday cake, and everyone shouts, "Make a wish." It wasn't King Solomon's birthday and he had no candles to blow out, but even God said, "Make a wish" (2 Chronicles 1:7-10). God, too, must be on the side of wishing.

But God sets limits to our wishing. And that's what the Ninth and Tenth Commandments are about. He warns that we may wish so much for (or covet) something that belongs to someone else that in the end we may steal it from him. So, God says, don't even wish for it.

Let's talk about three kinds of wishing:
- ❖ wishing that is wrong
- ❖ wishing that is foolish and futile
- ❖ wishing that is right

The first is that kind of wishing which the Lord puts on the no-no list. Your friend has a boyfriend, and you'd like him to be yours. But if he were yours, he couldn't be hers. So, stop wishing. Do nothing to take him away from her, even if you could.

After a while they may tire of each other and go their separate ways. Then you can wish, and if he is attracted to you, you are not taking him away from anyone.

Or let us suppose that you want the coach to pick you to be the pitcher, but he picks another player and has you be the catcher. At this point you may be tempted to hope that the pitcher will botch the game and give you a chance. As his catcher, you may actually give him less support than you should. This kind of wishing, God says, is wrong.

If you wish for money or power or popularity, it could be that in the long run someone else will have to have less money or power or popularity. Ambition is a good thing, if it does not crowd someone else off the field. Competition is good, up to a point. But if in competing for something you become unfair to someone else, if instead of helping him you crush him, then competition is no longer a good thing.

Success in business or politics has sometimes been this kind of ruthless, heartless, and cruel game. This kind of wishing (ambition which is coveting) may lead to deceit, to cunning, and to outright stealing, even if it often is technically within the law. It can also result in the thing you want becoming an idol, replacing God as the most important thing in your life.

The second kind of wishing is that which is simply foolish. If you are short and everyone in your family is short, it's silly to spend time wishing you were six foot three. If you can't run fast, try as you will, what sense is there in wishing that you could run one hundred meters in ten seconds? If you are an average student, even when you study hard, don't sit around wishing you were an Einstein. God has given you good, adequate equipment, so don't waste your time wishing you were someone else.

But there is a kind of wishing that is both right and good, the kind of wishing that God hopes you will do, the kind of wishing that will never take anything away from others. When God asked the young king, Solomon, to make a wish, and Solomon wished for wisdom instead of riches, God was very pleased. God could give Solomon all kinds of wisdom without taking wisdom away from anyone else.

Perhaps a person is rich, not because he has many things, but because he has few needs. To wish for things is a kind of disease, a spreading infection. The more you get, the more you want. To wish for wisdom and love and hope and mercy is of God. The more of this you get, the more it will spill over into the lives of others. Everyone will be the richer.

What do you mean by having only a few needs?

Ask yourself, what really do you need? You need food, but not pheasant under glass. You need clothes, but how many, really? You need shelter from the cold or heat—one room might do. You need safety so that you're not in danger of being attacked around every corner. Now, what else do you need? Think hard. Is there anything else you absolutely must have?

Surely no one believes that this is enough?

In Bangladesh or India they may. Millions of people don't have even this much. Hunger is the stark enemy of their lives, every day. In many countries, especially in the Western world, we are so accustomed to having these basic needs that we hardly think of them. We keep adding to the list, and think that we have all sorts of additional needs—motorbikes, cars, radios, televisions, telephones, boats, huge savings accounts, large salaries. There is no end to the list.

If it is wrong to covet, is it wrong for poor nations to covet some of our wealth?

Rightly or wrongly, they do. Both rich and poor covet. Poor nations throughout the world naturally want a bigger, more equitable share of the world's resources. We who are of the have nations are under our Lord's solemn judgment to find ways to help the have-not nations to obtain a fairer share (see Luke 3:11). Jesus did say, "To whom much is given, of him shall much be required" (Luke 12:48). While we enjoy our plenty in the midst of a world of want, we dare not close our ears to the distant thunder of God's judgment, "I was hungry and you gave me no food" (Matthew 25:42).

How about people in our own land? Is it wrong for them to want more?

Hardly. They certainly will try to better their condition. And, at its best, our government does try to distribute the wealth of our land more equitably through taxation and various programs of education, health, and welfare. Unfortunately, the gap between the rich and the poor is still disturbingly wide and seems to grow wider. Greed is deeply entrenched in human nature. The strong and the rich often keep pushing for more.

What can the average person do about the gap?

People who have exaggerated notions of what they ought to have or to earn can cut back, scale down desires and demands, and make it possible for others to have a fairer share. They can support governmental leaders in programs of taxation and aid that create better controls and distribution. Through church and volunteer organizations they can be of direct aid to people in need. And of course if they know specific people in want, they can go to their aid.

Isn't this a turnabout? Now I seem to be wishing or coveting for others and not for myself.

It's a glorious turnabout. Now you have struck on the secret of Christian life. By this kind of wishing you will find greater joy than almost any wishing you may do for yourself.

For reflection

1. Read 1 Corinthians 12 where the apostle, in an intriguing picture, warns that the ear should not wish it were an eye. Then read Chapter 13, where he rhapsodizes on love.

2. What do you "wish" for above everything else? Which of the three types of wishes is it?

3. What do these commands have to do with personal stewardship—that is, how we spend our time and our treasures?

The Apostle's Creed

13

More Than a Creator

The First Article

It boggles the mind to say, "I believe in God the Father."

We are in fact saying that there is a being, someone we call God, who like a great watchmaker made a huge watch called the universe, with billions of bodies plunging and circling around in billions of light-years of space, with amazing order and precision. We say further that he colonized one of these bodies, a very tiny island called earth, with his family. We are his daughters and sons. To us he is not only a god, not only a creator. He is our Father!

The author of a psalm poses the question, "When I look at your heavens . . . what are human beings. . . ? Yet you have made them a little lower than God . . ." (Psalm 8). It is a miracle that we can believe this at all.

The mathematician and the astronomer can describe the wonders of the universe for us. The botanist can tell us about the staggering variety and structures of trees and plants and flowers. The biologist can picture for us the amazing organization of an animal or human body. These scientists are all like remarkable photographers who tell us how it is. Only God can go beyond this scientific photography to tell us that human beings are his own special children.

As God's children, we are like God, created in his image. Although that image has been obscured by sin, we are more like God than like other animals. Biologists can do no more than tell us how much like other animals we are. In the Bible alone are we told that we are created in the likeness of God (Genesis 1:27). Without this incredible news, we could do no more than take our place at the peak of the pyramid of all animal life. We are after all more complex than monkeys or dogs. But with the Bible message, we take our place alongside of God, in his family. The earth, even the universe itself, is our Father's home and ours.

God does not claim me as his child because I think like him, nor because I do what he does, nor because I acknowledge him as my Father. I can forget about him—many do. He still claims me as his child. I can run away from him and never be with him again, either here or hereafter. He will grieve and say, "I have lost my child." And I will be a lost child throughout eternity.

The Bible tells us many things about God. Most importantly, it tells us that God loves you and me (see 1 John 4:10). He also loves truth and holiness and justice and mercy. He loves order and beauty. He has a terrible anger against all wickedness, because sin, whether our own or other's, hurts his children.

To warn us and guard us against what may hurt or destroy us, he has made rules. He made them for the planets and tides and oceans. He made them for the birds and fish. And he made rules for us, his children.

The planets and the fish cannot disobey the rules. God keeps them in complete control. Only you and I, his children, can disobey. To us alone of all his creation did he give the gift of freedom. He wants us to love him and obey him because we want to, not because (like the tides) we have to. After all, he is a father. He doesn't want his family to be like an army camp or a zoo.

It is the disobedience of God's children that brings on the major troubles of the world. Things go wrong when we no longer love God and one another. We become a family torn apart, selfish, fighting with one another and forgetting to care for either God or for each other.

Jesus Christ, God the Son, came to the world to try to put us together again into one great family.

I have a hard time believing the creation story in Genesis 1–2.

If you do, try thinking of the story not as a newspaper report, but as a great epic or poem through which we learn great truths: that God created all things, and that people are the high point of his creation. Don't worry too much about the details.

How is God like me, or how am I like him?

Of course he is not exactly like you, nor are you exactly like him. He is not confined to time and place as you are. But he is a person, or like a person. He is more than a force, like electricity or wind. He is enough like you so that you can talk to him in prayer, and so that he can talk to you through his Word.

Why is God pictured like a father and not a mother?

God is not an object, like a tree, so he couldn't very well call himself an *it*. Would there be any gain for us if God were to have been revealed or described as a mother-God? Could it not be that a thoroughly loving father would have the qualities of tenderness normally attributed to mothers, and in addition have the strength normally associated with fathers? No demeaning of motherhood was intended, surely, when Jesus taught us to pray, "Our Father, who art in heaven."

How can we best thank God?

A good place to begin may be in church. Aware of God's great goodness in creating and redeeming you to be his child, you come Sunday after Sunday to thank and praise him. Your praise of God, of course, can be a continuous melody in your heart—as you awaken in the morning, as you walk through the wood, as you work, as you eat, as you study, and as you fall asleep at night (see Psalm 103).

If I really want to serve God, do I become a pastor, a teacher, a missionary, or some kind of full-time worker in the church?

You certainly may, and God calls many to such service. But God's workshop is a big one. Each of us is enlisted to tell the story of God's love, by word and life-style, whatever occupation we have. You need not be a "professional" to do that. Moreover, everything is God's, and in the care of farms, schools, industries, hospitals, and governments, we are taking care of things for him. Remember that Jesus pointed us especially to one another and said that whatever we did for anyone in need we were in effect doing for him.

What difference is there between serving God in a religious job and some other occupation?

Probably none, as long as you are doing what you believe God wants you to do. If you are a nurse or a doctor taking care of the bodies of people, your care of them is no less "religious" or "of God" than that of the pastor who prays at the person's bedside. Luther once pointed out that the person who sweeps a floor is serving God, not because he sings a hymn while he sweeps, but because he sweeps the floor clean. When we do any honorable task well and out of a desire to serve God and his creation, we are actually serving God (Colossians 3:17).

Do I serve God to please him or to obey him?

Both. You cannot separate the two. You seek to please God by obeying him, and in obeying him you please him. You do both because you are God's child.

For reflection

1. Read Matthew 6:25-34 for Jesus' beautiful description of the Father's care of his children.

2. Not all earthly fathers (or mothers, for that matter) show love to their children. Does it bother you to think of or address God as "Father?"

3. What questions do you have about God?

14

Managing the Planet

The First Article

God turned over the management of the planet to his children. He said, "Have dominion," take care of it (Genesis 1:28). God is still around to instruct and to correct his children, and to step in when things get out of hand. But the management is ours.

Our record is not too good. At one point, at the time of Noah, God almost closed the business, but not quite. He decided to continue with his children in the executive and managerial role until such time as Christ would return to usher in "the new heaven and the new earth."

When God entrusted the world to Adam and Eve, the business was in perfect condition—no weak spots and no debts. Anything that has gone wrong with the world is not of God, but the outcome of our mismanagement.

As far back as we have historical records, the human race has been both a builder and a destroyer. It may be difficult to measure how well we have built. The population has expanded many times over. Continents have been explored and developed. One secret after another in nature has been uncovered and put to use. People have not been idle. And now we have begun to explore other worlds.

But every now and then our world has exploded into violence and destruction. The years are littered with wars, those of the twentieth century most devastating of all. Nor has the record of our getting along with other members of the family been encouraging. Member against member, tribe against tribe, nation against nation, race against race—this has been a continuing pattern.

It would not be difficult to conclude that human beings are more often destroyers than builders. At times we are like a child who laboriously and patiently builds a castle of blocks, and having looked at it awhile, on a momentary impulse kicks it all over the living room floor.

Despite these destructive spasms, our race has expanded the enterprise so much that demand may now exceed supply. If we are not careful in using what we have, and if God does not unlock new secrets about available resources, there may not be enough food, enough clean air and water, enough energy to support the race.

The Western world has been the most enterprising in developing the resources of the earth and most extravagant in consuming these same resources. The outcome of human life on this planet rests in no small measure on how our part of the family now manages the power and the wealth it controls.

God took a big risk in making us his children and putting us here. He took another risk when as God the Son he came personally to become a part of the enterprise and to bail us out of an impossible situation by dying on a cross for us. What a staggering maneuver of love and trust!

If we will but understand God's own stake in us and in the world and comprehend even in part the love he has for us, out of sheer gratitude to him we may yet have the wisdom and the will to care for God's earth and for one another, so that our grandchildren will possess some of the good life God has planned for his children.

Do human beings have the capacity to destroy the world?

Scientists tell us that we have the capacity in nuclear bombs and in poisonous chemicals to kill off every living thing on the earth. This is a relatively new situation. With the competitive stockpiling of nuclear warheads beginning in the 1950s, the world became aware that the old days of swords, spears, gunpowder, and even nitroglycerin were changed. The issue of world peace is the supreme issue of our time, the international issue to dwarf all others.

Why did God let us discover atomic energy and dangerous chemicals?

Both atomic energy and these chemicals, properly used, can be of immeasurable help in making a better world. If God were to have blocked out people's minds from discovering anything dangerous, we probably today would not have electricity, cars, or airplanes. It is evidence of God's love for us that he puts these resources in the world and gives to us, his children, the probing minds to find them.

Did earlier generations manage the world better than we do now?

Probably not. A sober reading of history will show that no age has been without mismanagement. The differences today may be that the business has become much more complex than before and requires of us greater skills than were demanded earlier. People were probably no better and no worse in the first century than in the twentieth. A study of history will probably make us neither pessimistic nor optimistic. I tend personally to be on the optimistic side. The effect of Christ's kingdom in our midst has produced magnificent movements for the care of the poor and oppressed.

What is God's chief concern in this world?

That his children grow to be more like him in love and joy (see 1 Timothy 2:4). God is not satisfied that we merely survive, or that we invent new and more dazzling gadgets. At the same time he does want us to care for each other so that we all have the basic necessities, such as food and clothing. Jesus, who came to die for the souls of God's children, was almost harsh in his insistence that we help one another with these elemental needs. He said that in feeding a hungry person we would in effect be feeding him.

If food and fresh water may be in short supply for the world, isn't the problem so great that nothing I do will matter?

It may seem to matter little. It will take united action by the great governments of the world. But such action will require a change in the attitudes of people, and that's where you and I can help. We can at least stop living as if there'll always be enough (see Philippians 4:11-12).

To shift from an economy that is virtually built on people buying and using more than they need to one of cautious use of the world's supply will be complicated and will require great care in planning. It appears that it must be done.

Even if we take good care of the world's supplies, can we hope that life on the earth will be improved for us in the future?

I certainly hope so. If by "improved" you mean more food and things, probably not. But, if you mean a better distribution of food and things, and if you mean a world where nations have learned to live together with less warfare, then the answer is yes. And this could be a better world than we have ever known. Scientists in general are optimistic in their belief that the very technology that threatens us will be turned to the solution of many of the problems that loom before us. The God who made us his children and who let his only Son be our Brother and Savior has promised not to abandon us. Our hope ultimately rests in him.

For reflection

1. Read Isaiah 11:1-9 for a vision of the effect of the coming of Christ into the affairs of people and of nations.

2. In your opinion, what is the biggest challenge we face in the world today? How can Christian people respond to this challenge?

15

Your Father's House

The First Article

You may look at the universe in four different ways.

You may think of it as a madhouse, where injustice and tragedy and death strike without any design. It's a crazy world. There are no built-in values, no right and wrong, no good and evil—only a jumble.

Or you may think of it as a machine, a cold, beautiful, heartless machine. How it got going, no one knows. The wheels keep turning. You are just a cog. You do what you do because you are driven by forces you cannot control. You are as helpless to change things, or yourself, as the tides are to stop their ebb and flow.

Or you may think of it as a vast courtroom, where everyone gets what he has coming, no more and no less. If a woman is born blind, she had it coming. If a suicide airplane levels buildings in New York, New York deserved it.

Or you can think of this universe and the world as your Father's house. God, my Father, built the house, put me in it, keeps it in repair, and in it "provides me with food and clothing, home and family, daily work, and all I need from day to day. God also protects me in time of danger and guards me from every evil" (*The Small Catechism*). This is how the Bible pictures the universe.

Perhaps you are wondering: If this is God's house, why doesn't God manage it better? Why is there sin and tragedy and death? Is God too busy with the stars to watch over his little earth and to take care of us, his children?

In some matters you can clearly see that God manages well. He provides sunshine and rain, the seasons, plants and animals and minerals—in fact, everything we need for this body and life. If we were wise enough and good enough to distribute goods equitably, all people the world over could probably have enough. It is the ignorance and selfishness of people that interfere with God's management.

In many ways that we cannot see, God is still in charge. He does not let human sins and destruction get altogether out of hand. He captures the minds and hearts of many people, and they pit themselves against the evil of the world. Good fights against evil, love against hatred, honesty against corruption. The evil forces may try to get possession of the Father's house, but they will fail. They will trouble the life of the house, but they cannot take it from the Father.

God also forces evil to destroy itself. A dishonest public official, for instance, who becomes wealthy on bribes and extortion becomes the envy of other dishonest people who covet his ill-gotten gains and who then plot his destruction. Destroying him, they in turn become candidates for the same wretched sequence of destruction. Nations that lust for power are finally overcome by other nations that lust for power.

There is little comfort in thinking that history is the grim story of one bad person destroying another bad person. But there is reassurance in the fact that the forces for good can at times find themselves in a strange partnership with evil itself in administering justice. God does not let evil have its own way in his house.

We live in troublesome times. (Most likely this has been true of every age.) Sometimes it seems that evil has the upper hand and will take over. There is corruption in governments of the world, greed among the people of power and wealth and indeed among most people, indifference to moral values in every level of society, and crime and violence and threat of war. Is God himself up to keeping order in his house?

We believe that in strange and often unobserved ways God is at work to keep his house. We dare not lose confidence in the One who made and redeemed us and who gave us this home.

Everybody seems worried about the future. Should we be?

How can you help it? Anxiety and worry have been par for the course in every generation. Jesus addressed his worrying friends, "O you of little faith," and told them not to fear for the tomorrows

(Matthew 6:25-34). No doubt we shall continue to worry, but knowing that the tomorrows are not only in our bungling hands but in God's mighty hands, we can approach the future with panic and paralysis kept in check.

Does God bless the good people more than the bad people?

Yes, although this is not always clearly seen. He gives rain and sunshine to all alike. In a war, both good and bad people die. But in the midst of hardship, people who try to obey God do open their hearts and minds to God's blessings. The apostle Paul, who certainly had his share of trouble and pain, said, "We know that in everything God works for good with those who love him" (Romans 8:28).

Sometimes it seems that bad people prosper more than good people, doesn't it?

At times it certainly appears so. A man defrauds his neighbor. With this money he takes his family on a vacation to Spain, while his neighbor is unable to make payments on his house and car and loses them. It seems that it is the thief who prospers. He may get caught, of course, and go to prison. And even if he is never caught, he has to live with the fear of being discovered. Without that fear, he still lives with an uneasy conscience that never gives him joy.

Can we always know what good God is working out for us?

No, sometimes what we think is bad for us may actually be good. A woman watched a bee fly in through an open window and try to find its way out. It dashed its little body against one window pane after another, missing the one open space. The woman picked up a towel and tried to guide the bee's flight toward freedom. But the bee, not understanding, thought her an enemy and hurled itself against the towel and buzzed around the room in panic. At long last the woman succeeded in maneuvering the creature to the open window and suddenly the bee, sensing the sunshine and trees, flew into the wide open world to which it belonged. God sometimes uses circumstances that we think are bad to move us towards doors or windows that may be for our real good.

If God protects us, does he also punish us?

Yes, but God is more like a great and good father than like a judge. A good parent will punish a child because he or she loves the child. In Hebrews 12:6, we are told ". . . the Lord disciplines him whom he loves, and chastises (punishes) every son whom he receives." Instinctively we know that God disciplines us because God loves and cares for us. In this way, God is like a good, although firm, parent.

For reflection

1. Read Psalm 91 and note the extravagant imagery in this beautiful poem about God's care of his children.

2. Have you experienced discipline or punishment that led to learning or growth? Explain.

3. What is your reaction to the idea expressed by the Apostle Paul that everything works for good for those who trust God?

16

Who Is Jesus?

The Second Article

Of all the people who have ever lived on earth, Jesus is in a class by himself. A billion people carry his name. Millions of churches and cathedrals have been built for him. All other great persons—the Caesars, the disciples, Napoleon, Lincoln—take their silent places on library shelves and do not bother us. But Jesus rose from the dead and is with us always.

Yet he was one of us. As a baby he no doubt cried, nursed, drooled, wet his diapers, caught colds—like any other baby. As a boy growing up in a small town, he probably roamed the hills, caught snakes and frogs, played games, helped in his father's carpentry shop—like any other boy. Once at the age of twelve, he wandered into the Jerusalem temple and amazed the scholars with the questions he asked.

Nothing much is recorded of his life until he was about thirty years old. Then he left home, traveling about from village to village.

Soon others began walking with him—Peter, John, Andrew, James, and others. He preached, he taught, he healed the sick, he befriended the poor. Before long it was clear that there was something different about Jesus.

When he spoke, there was a strange authority about what he said, unlike other teachers and preachers. He told wonderful stories. He did amazing feats for people, like making the blind to see. Even nature seemed to obey him: he changed water to wine, he walked on the sea, he stilled the storm. Sometimes his speech puzzled people, as when he called himself the Way and the Truth and the Life, when he forgave sins, and when he indicated that he and the Father were one. Yet many people followed him.

One day he announced that he was going to Jerusalem and that he would die there. His disciples tried to stop him. They were bewildered when he told them that it was necessary for him to die if God's plans were to be realized.

And he did die. He was crucified. His friends buried him. But he did not stay in the grave. The third day he arose from death. To begin with, his closest friends couldn't believe it. But they saw him and even ate with him many times. Then one day, about forty days after his resurrection, he was carried away in a cloud. He had gone back to heaven.

Before going, he told his followers that although they would no longer be seeing him around, he would still be with them in a very real and powerful way.

His followers believed him and set out to win the world for him. They told people what he had said and done. Before long, they also began telling people who he was. He was God, God the Son, come to earth! But he was man too, every inch a man like all other men, except without sin. How he could be God and man at the same time, no one has really been able either to understand or explain. But for two thousand years countless people around the world have believed him.

Whom did his disciples believe Jesus to be?

At first, most likely they thought of him as a great teacher and prophet. Gradually, however, they saw that he was different from other prophets. Once, when Jesus asked them, "Who do you say that I am?" Peter answered, "The Christ of God" (Luke 9:20). After the resurrection, Thomas, feeling Jesus' hands and feet, burst out, "My Lord and my God" (John 20:28). The clearest statement of belief is by John, who calls Jesus the Word and says ". . . and the Word was God" (John 1:1). At some point the disciples remembered that an angel had told his mother, Mary, before he was born that his name should be Jesus (Savior) because he would save his people from their sins.

What did Jesus do that indicated he was God?

He forgave sins, which only God can do (Matthew 9:2; Mark 2:5; Luke 5:20; Luke 7:48).

Did Jesus himself claim to be God?

Yes. He said, "I and the Father are one" (John 10:30), and "Know that I am in my Father" (John 14:20). In Matthew 1:23, which refers to a prophecy from Isaiah 7:14, he is called Emmanuel, which means "God with us."

If the disciples had not believed him to be God, what would have happened?

Probably nothing. They certainly would not have spread out over the world at great risk and suffering to win disciples for Jesus if he had been only another great man like Abraham or Moses.

Had the disciples expected God to come to earth?

They did believe the prophesies, the promises of God that some day the Messiah, the Anointed One, would come, sent from God to deliver them. They did not quite understand what he would be like when he came. Many thought he would be a human leader who would free them from the rule of oppressive nations like Rome. It was years later that Paul said that "In Christ God was reconciling the world to himself" (2 Corinthians 5:19).

Does the Bible say explicitly that Jesus is both God and man?

Yes. There is no other way to understand John (1:14) when he says, "And the Word became flesh and dwelt among us." And Paul, in Philippians 2:6-8, says of Jesus, "Though he was in the form of God . . . (he) emptied himself, taking the form of a servant, being born in the likeness of men. . . . being found in human form he humbled himself and became obedient unto death, even death on a cross," and concludes by saying that "at the name of Jesus every knee should bow, in heaven and on earth and under the earth, and every tongue confess that Jesus Christ is Lord. . . ."

Is it important to us that Jesus was human?

Yes. Only as a human being could he die, and he died for us. It is also of great comfort when we pray to him to remember that Jesus himself knows personally what it is like to be tempted and to suffer. In Hebrews 4:14 we are reassured, "Since then we have a great high priest who has passed through the heavens, Jesus, the Son of God, let us hold fast our confession. For we have not a high priest who is unable to sympathize with our weakness, but one who in every respect has been tempted as we are, yet without sin."

Christ's humanity is also important when we ask what it means to be human. Who is the model? Whom are we to be like, if we are to be persons, real persons? By becoming one of us, Jesus (God the Son) has given the greatest possible worth to being a human being. We are not mere cousins of the rat; we are brothers and sisters of Christ.

Where do we find the best summaries of who Jesus is?

In the three great ecumenical creeds of the church: the Apostles' Creed, the Nicene Creed, and the longer Athanasian Creed. The first two are in most Christian hymnbooks, and are included in orders of service, the liturgies of the church. Every Christian should know these two from memory.

For reflection

1. Read Colossians 1:15-20 and think about the person and the power of Jesus.

2. How would you describe Jesus to someone who was not familiar with the Christian faith?

17

Conquerors with Christ

The Second Article

Why did Jesus come to the earth? God's children were held captive in a vast concentration camp, that's why. He had to wage war against the enemy. He had to batter down the gates of the camp and open the cells to set his people free.

Warfare is one picture the Bible uses to tell us why Jesus had to come. Another picture is a courtroom. The next chapter will take us to this courtroom.

Imagine yourself in a concentration camp. You are a prisoner. The enemy captured you and threw you into a cell. There he brainwashes you, so that you forget your family and no longer remember what a world of freedom is like. There is no window in the cell, and gradually you come to like darkness better than light. In fact, you would be afraid of the light.

Day after day you sit there, or lie on your mat, or walk a few steps in the cell. You eat the food pushed through your door. You get used to this routine. You are not happy, but you have at least forgotten to want anything else.

You could never get out on your own. In fact, you no longer think of trying. You would stay there until you die, unless someone from the outside came and fought the enemy and defeated him and broke open the door of your cell.

This is what Jesus did. Go back to the Genesis story in the Bible. When Adam and Eve chose to obey the enemy of God (Satan), they and all people after them slipped away from God and came under the control of Satan. He had no love for them, so he threw them into his prison. He then brainwashed them and made them think that the darkness of the cell was better and more natural than the sunshine of freedom. In fact, they virtually forgot what light was like.

Satan convinced them that they were happy with half-truths, with passing pleasures, with money that couldn't buy either joy or peace. He made them use other people instead of loving them. He twisted their values around so that they thought life was the business of taking care of themselves and not being concerned about others.

In spite of Satan's cunning, in spite of the way people became adjusted to the dimness of the prison, it was a lonely place. Everyone lived for himself and to himself.

Jesus came to change all that. He pitted himself against what had become a triple-headed enemy: Satan, people's own selfishness, and the ways of the prison, that is, the ways of the world.

Jesus could not change all this simply by giving lectures on freedom and by showing people how they should live. It took more than a school. It took a war. He had to destroy the enemy. And that cost him his life on a cross.

This happened some two thousand years ago. The power of the triple-enemy is now broken, the doors of the prison are shattered, the Father's home is now wide open to us, and we are free to return to God and to live his kind of life. The apostle Paul cried, "Thanks be to God, who gives us the victory through our Lord Jesus Christ" (1 Corinthians 15:57).

It is of critical importance that we believe this. Otherwise we might go on living as if we were prisoners still. When Napoleon's army was destroyed by the Russian winter, messengers came to central Europe with the good news that people no longer had to take orders from Napoleon's captains. They were free again. But there were some cities that did not believe the messengers. They kept on living as slaves of Napoleon, even though Napoleon's power was broken.

We too might continue to live as slaves if we don't believe that Christ has defeated our enemies. But if we do believe, we shall start living with God, free to turn from our selfish and unworthy ways, to grow day to day into the freedom of living for God and for one another.

That's great news, and I want to believe it. But I have a hard time feeling very much like a victor.

Don't worry about feelings. God doesn't ask you to feel anything. He only asks that you believe the news, that you assume that you have a right to claim this release from prison and this freedom, and that you thank him.

Is that really all?

Yes. But you are not free in a vacuum. You don't leave the prison and simply stand outside of the walls, bewildered and confused. You'll now hear a call, the call of God's Spirit to enter the Father's house where there is joy, where there are tasks waiting and a whole new lifestyle beckoning (Galatians 5:13). You are no longer under the old tyranny. In the new atmosphere selfishness, lust, loneliness, and fear will loosen their grip on you. You can be a victor in fact as well as by faith.

If I still fail, then what?

You may fail (in fact, you certainly will), but you are a victor still—remember that. Christ's victory has become yours. The habits of the prison, especially our deep self-centeredness, are stubborn. They will hang on, in one form or another, until you die. The ways of freedom are not easily mastered either. But within the Father's house, a lot of forces are going for us—primarily God himself, but also others who have been freed, other Christians. You are not alone in the struggles for a life of freedom.

A life of freedom isn't necessarily easy, then?

No. In many ways the life in prison is easier. Bishop Hanns Lilje of Germany, a prisoner in a Nazi camp during the great war, once commented that in some ways prison is the nicest place, because there you don't have to make any decisions. Even your menu is decided for you. It is when you get out of prison and are free again that you have responsibilities, accountability, and important tasks to do. But isn't that what makes freedom wonderful?

Apparently freedom doesn't mean that I do what I want to do, does it?

Real freedom never means freedom to do what you jolly well want to do. In a profound sense, it means freedom to do what you *ought* to do. In prison, before you knew Christ, you were so brainwashed that you thought you were doing what you wanted to do. You thought it was natural and even fun to be selfish and greedy and immoral and dishonest. Now, out of prison, you understand that this was not freedom at all. To be really free is to do what God intended you to do. And God works changes in us so that we begin to want to do, and actually enjoy doing, what he wants.

But don't I have to obey God? It strikes me that obedience is not the same as freedom.

Strange as it seems, this is freedom. Try it. When you get outside of yourself and become concerned about God's will and the needs and wants of other people, as God commands, you discover that when you're no longer all tied up in your own self-concerns, self-defense, and self-pity, this really is freedom (see Romans 6:16-23).

You're connecting this kind of freedom with the cross of Christ?

Yes, it was the death and resurrection of Jesus, this gigantic maneuver of God in defeating the powers that held us in bondage, that set us free.

For reflection

1. Read Romans 8 and note the many aspects of this freedom Christ has won for us.

2. What is your reaction to the idea that Christ's death frees us from a kind of prison?

3. Which of the three "heads" of the triple-headed enemy (p. 67) is most powerful? Why? How does Jesus' forgiveness defeat these enemies?

18

Guilty—but Free

The Second Article

We have discussed warfare as one picture the Bible uses to tell us why Jesus came. Now let's look at the biblical picture of the courtroom.

If you are arrested and brought into court, the judge will ask you, "How do you plead, guilty or not guilty?" If you are found guilty, you face punishment; if not, you will be set free.

Let us imagine the most supreme court of all—God's court. You and I stand before God's bench, charged with being sinners. The law of the court says, "The wages (penalty) of sin is death."

The judge asks how we plead. We have no choice. We are all guilty. Each of us is a sinful human being. All have fallen short. We have disobeyed God, broken his law, both by the evil we have done and by the good we neglected to do.

Kindhearted as the judge may be, he has no choice. He must convict us and sentence us. The sentence is death.

Then an utterly strange thing happens. The judge, who is Jesus Christ, steps down from the bench, and takes our sentences upon himself. He exchanged places with us. We receive his righteousness and he receives our sins. And we are free—no sentence, no prison, no death. We receive forgiveness. The Bible has described what happens by saying that we are justified by grace alone through faith in Jesus.

This is an unbelievable turn of events. How can someone else, Jesus Christ, take the responsibility and the punishment for our sins? And how can his death on the cross wipe out my sins, along with yours, and the sins of the whole world? How can forgiveness be that sweeping and complete? There is really no way to explain this. We can only accept it, believe it, count on it, and start to thank Christ.

Now some of the great promises of the Bible begin to ring in our ears and make our hearts sing for joy. The promises are both in the Old Testament and in the New: "Though your sins are like scarlet, they shall be white as snow" (Isaiah 1:18); "Comfort my people, says your God. Speak tenderly to Jerusalem, and cry to her that her . . . iniquity is pardoned" (Isaiah 40:2); "If thou, O Lord, shouldst mark iniquities, Lord, who shall stand? But there is forgiveness with thee" (Psalms 130:3-4); "As far as the east is from the west, so far does he remove our transgressions from us" (Psalms 103:12); "There is therefore now no condemnation for those who are in Christ Jesus" (Romans 8:1); "God in Christ forgave you" (Ephesians 4:32).

A missionary in China years ago became a close friend of a Buddhist priest. Each learned much from the other. One day the missionary asked his friend, "Is there something the Christian religion offers that the Buddhist religion does not have?" After a long silence, the priest answered, "The forgiveness of sins."

If a poll were taken among all the Christians of the world and the question were asked, "What one thing does Christ give you above all else?" the answer would surely be "the forgiveness of sins." All the other blessings of God, like little streams, flow from the one central spring, which is forgiveness. Luther once said, "Where there is forgiveness of sin, there is life and salvation." And it is Christ's death and resurrection some two thousand years ago that make it possible for us to be forgiven.

What does God take into consideration when he judges us?

He looks at our deeds, to be sure, but even more he examines our hearts, our secret thoughts, desires, and motives. He looks at the wrongs we have done, and at all the good we might have done but failed to do. Add all this together, and all of us face a staggering need for forgiveness.

I don't like to think of Jesus as a judge. I want him as a friend.

He is both. When you face him in the high court, he must of course condemn you. You are guilty. But when you stand at the foot of the cross, he is there to die for you as a friend and save you. He is both your judge and Savior.

Isn't a religion that hands out forgiveness this freely too easy?

Forgiveness is not easy for our Lord. He died to make forgiveness possible. Suppose you can't swim and you are drowning in deep water. Someone leaps in and saves you, but is caught in the currents and drowns. He dies and you live. It cost Jesus his life to save you (John 15:13).

To be forgiven is not easy even for you. You will already have changed radically when you recognize your need for forgiveness. To be deeply sorry is one of the hardest things to do. To be in the position of having to receive mercy from someone else, as an undeserving beggar, goes against every instinct of pride we have. To throw ourselves upon the mercy of God is to enter the door to a whole new world—a world where you love and forgive, as you are loved and forgiven. A religion of forgiveness is not an easy religion.

But it doesn't seem fair. Shouldn't I have to pay for my own sins?

It isn't fair. If God were only fair and gave you what you have coming, no more and no less, then you would have to pay with your life. But God's mercy swallows up what we would call fair. He loves and loves, and he forgives and forgives. There is no end to his mercy.

But does not God punish sin at all?

Yes, he does. He has arranged his world in such a way that if people disobey him and go their selfish ways, their sins do catch up with them. If you overeat or go to drugs, you suffer. If you break the speed limit and have a smashup and end up in the hospital, you suffer. If in unfaithfulness or indifference you let your marriage go on the rocks, you and many others suffer. Christ's forgiveness does not save you from punishment or suffering. But his forgiveness saves you from the worst of all punishments and suffering, which is to be thrown away from God. You turn to be forgiven, and he always takes you and holds you in his great love.

Isn't there something, some little thing, for me to do, before he can love me and forgive me?

Is there some little thing you must do before your mother will love you? Would your mother say, "Mary, I will love you if you're good, or if you want me to love you?" Even more than a mother's love, God's love and forgiveness are simply there. They are yours! You can't stop God from being loving and forgiving any more than you can stop the sun from shining. You can keep the sunshine from reaching you by pulling the blinds or by refusing to come out of a cave. But the sun keeps on shining, regardless of what you do.

When we are told, "Repent, for the kingdom of heaven is at hand" (Matthew 4:17), it is as if a voice is saying, "Turn around! A whole world of love and forgiveness wants to claim you." Even to turn around, or to repent, you will need God's help (see Ephesians 2:1). But he is more than eager to help, if we give him the nod.

For reflection

1. Read Isaiah 55 and reflect on how God deals with us when we come to him in repentance and need.

2. God's forgiveness removes the guilt of our sin, but we often still "feel" the effects of guilt. If we have harmed another person, besides asking for God's forgiveness, how can we seek to "feel" less guilty?

3. How is Jesus both judge and liberator?

19

Ruler of All

The Second Article

Studdert Kennedy, a British World War I chaplain, was visiting a captain who was recovering from what had seemed certain death. He said, "Padre, tell me what God is like. Whenever I've been transferred from one regiment to another, my first question has always been 'What's the colonel like?' because I've discovered that conditions in the regiment will be what the colonel makes them. Before the war, when taking a position with a new firm, I'd ask, 'What's the boss like?' Now I'm told I'll recover, and I must know what the Big Boss of life is like."

Jesus is the "Big Boss" of life. He himself announced, "All authority in heaven and on earth has been given to me" (Matthew 28:18). He is the ruler of the universe. In the language of the Nicene Creed he is "God of God, Light of Light, Very God of very God." He is God in every sense of the word.

Sometimes Jesus is called our high priest, sometimes our prophet, sometimes our king. In the Old Testament the high priest offered the sacrifices (oxen, goats, lambs, doves) for sin on behalf of the people. Jesus, as high priest, offered up himself as the one great sacrifice for the sins of the world. Also, in the Old Testament there were prophets who were teachers, telling of God and his will. Jesus, as prophet, not only taught us about God and his will, but revealed God to be himself, endless in love and mercy.

Jesus is not like other rulers, hidden within some well-protected office. He is at our elbows, nearer than the air we breathe, always ready to hear us and help us. He is at once a ruler and a friend. But let us not forget that he is the ruler, the king, of everything. He is the king who has come down into the created universe, down as a human being, and gone up again in his resurrection, pulling us up with him.

In the Gospels we meet him primarily as a friend, the man from Galilee who went about doing good. We meet him as the teacher. We meet him as one of us, dying on a cross. We may overlook that he is the ruler of the universe.

The story is told of a young king who made a tour through his kingdom. As he and his company passed through the streets of a village, his eye caught the eyes of a beautiful peasant girl. Back in his palace, he couldn't forget her. He had fallen in love with her.

Now, what should he do—go back to the village and ask her to be his wife, to become queen of the kingdom? He didn't dare do that. He thought to himself, "She will be shocked, overcome with awe, perhaps fear." But he didn't want her fear or her awe. He wanted her love.

So he disguised himself, came to the village as a peasant, lived and worked there, and won her love. Only then did he tell her that he was the king, and that in marrying him she would live in the castle as a queen.

Jesus came to the world as one of us. People loved him—as a man. Only gradually did his followers understand that he was more than a friend, that he was God come to earth, and that in following him they would live with him in his eternal kingdom.

It is to this kind of king we are called to commit our lives. When we pray to Jesus we are praying to one who controls the stars and galaxies. We are praying to one who is Lord of lords, King of kings, Son of God, who holds the whole universe in his hands. And the most precious part of that universe is people, the people for whom he died and whom he wants to have with him forever—you and me!

He is at the right hand of the Father, that is, the place of power. He is in our midst; he is within us. And one day in a burst of glory he will return for all to see him as he is.

Is Jesus so much different from other great people who have lived on earth?

Not at first glance, perhaps. He didn't try to be different. He came to be one of us.

But he was different, in his sinless life and especially in his resurrection! When the Holy Spirit had revealed to his followers who Jesus was, they began to tell the world that he was God the Son come to earth to save the world. And hundreds of millions have believed them.

But millions do not believe, do they?

No, many think the story too fantastic and do not believe. Others are afraid to believe and to have their lives changed. Still others have not heard about him yet. We are still under his command to go into all the world and tell the story and win people for him.

Dare we tell Buddhists, Hindus, Muslims, and others that Jesus is such a Lord?

We have no choice if we belong to Jesus. Many are glad to hear about him. A learned Hindu, hearing for the first time about Jesus, told E. Stanley Jones, a missionary to India, "I knew God had to be like that." Jesus meets the deepest yearnings and longings of the human spirit. He belongs to everyone, and everyone belongs to him.

Does this mean that Buddhism and other religions are all wrong?

No, God has revealed himself in some manner to them too, but not in his fullness. It remains for them to hear about Jesus as Lord to know God as friend and Savior. D. T. Niles, an eminent Christian evangelist from Ceylon, said that we must remember that Jesus, since he is Lord of all, is in these countries and religions in some manner, even before the missionaries come to tell them.

Peter said, "There is salvation in no one else" (Acts 4:12). Is that true?

We believe that only through the death and resurrection of Jesus is anyone saved. This may seem too radical a claim. How about people who have never heard of Jesus? It is not up to us to decide their fate. God alone knows how to judge them. Even they, however, if they are saved, are saved because Jesus has won the battle and has paid the price for them.

If Jesus is ruler, he must have rules for us, doesn't he?

Yes, he has rules. He has rules, or laws, for the winds and the tides, and he has rules for us. We alone of his creation can obey or disobey. His comprehensive rule is that we love God and that we love one another, as he has loved us (see Colossians 3:1-2).

Will there come a time when everyone will worship Jesus as Lord?

Some will go to their deaths without worshiping him. But there will come a day when everyone will recognize him as Lord, either joyfully or reluctantly. He will come in glory to preside over the final judgment and will usher in the new heaven and the new earth. Then we will know the truth of Paul's vision, "At the name of Jesus every knee should bow, in heaven and on earth . . . and every tongue confess that Jesus Christ is Lord" (Philippians 2:10-11).

For reflection

1. Read Revelation 21:1-7. This is the vision given us of the ultimate triumph of our King and the blessings that at last will be ours.

2. In a seminary class a student asked the instructor: "What about people who haven't heard about Jesus—will they be saved?" The instructor replied: "If you are concerned, go tell them." What do you think of this exchange?

20

God Is Here

The Third Article

God is around. That is the one, towering truth given us in the doctrine of the Holy Spirit. God did not create the world and us and then leave us to go our sinful ways. Our Lord did not die on a cross, rise again, and then retreat to some heavenly palace and forget about us. He did not establish his kingdom in our midst to have it unoccupied. God is here, powerfully at work among us. That's what we mean when we confess, "I believe in the Holy Spirit. . . ."

He is here to prod us into the kingdom prepared for us. Imagine, if you will, a beautiful lake. A friend frolicking in the water calls you to come in. You look wistfully on. You pick up courage to wade in. You get your toes wet, then your knees—but the water is cold and you're not much of a swimmer. But your friend keeps laughing and calling, "The water is wonderful out here." At last you plunge. You discover that the water is friendly, it holds you up. Before long you're having a rollicking time in the deep.

The Holy Spirit is the friend. He keeps calling you to come into the glories of God's kingdom. He tells you to stop shivering on the beach, to stop inching your way, and to leap into the deep—into the fullness of the kingdom, the kingdom which our Lord has designed and won for us. But you stand there still. Then he comes to take you by the hand and lead you into the deep.

Speaking of the Holy Spirit, Luther says, "I believe that I cannot by my own understanding or effort believe in Jesus Christ my Lord, or come to him. But the Holy Spirit has called me through the Gospel, enlightened me with his gifts, and sanctified and preserved me in the true faith."

He calls us. He calls us to listen to God, really listen, for what God has to say to us. Ever since we were old enough to listen, we've probably heard about God at home, in church school, in church services. But have we ever thought that God was talking especially to us—to me? The Word of God is not primarily *about* God; it is God singling out you and me, to say something to each of us. It is almost as if he takes you aside, away from everyone else, and says, "Now, my dear friend, I want a word with you alone. Listen to what I have to say."

Many people can tell you about moments like that:

"I was in a car accident. I saw the other car coming, and then there was a terrible crash. I lay in the hospital for weeks. It was then that I really listened for what God had to say to me."

"I was afraid of losing my job, and then one day the president of the company called me in and told me that I had been promoted. I couldn't have been more surprised, and suddenly I found myself thanking God."

"I remember when our son had turned against us, and I prayed and prayed for him. In my prayers for him, God turned me around to see myself, and for the first time I cried out for forgiveness—for myself."

"One Sunday something in the pastor's sermon seemed to jump out at me, and I knew God was calling me."

Whenever the Holy Spirit calls, he aims to have us see Christ, his judgment of our sins, and his forgiveness, and to lead us into his kingdom. We shall never come on our own. It is the work of the Holy Spirit in our hearts that makes us listen to our Lord and come to him.

Do people have to have something bad happen to them before they will listen?

No, they shouldn't. It is a strange thing, however, that it is when we are afraid or in trouble that we are mostly likely to listen to God. If God keeps on giving us good things, like health and friends and family, we ought then, more than in difficult times, to stop in our tracks to thank him and to ask him what he wants us to do with our lives (see Romans 2:4). He is waiting to tell us.

But it isn't always pleasant to hear what God has to say, is it?

Often it isn't. He points us to our shortcomings and our wrong-doings. He exposes our self-centeredness. We become ashamed and embarrassed over how seldom we have bothered to listen to him or thank him. Through the gospel, we know how wonderful he has been to us, to die on a cross for us. To face him and to listen may not be comfortable.

If your aunt, for instance, had given you a car so that you could get a job, and if you never bothered to thank her, and didn't even take the job but just ran around with her car for fun, to meet your aunt would not be pleasant.

God has given us good minds, good bodies, many opportunities to do good. If we never do anything worthwhile with all this, it will not be pleasant to hear what he has to say, if we stop to listen. And the Holy Spirit is intent on having us listen.

There is good news too, isn't there, if we stop to listen?

The best news in the world. Christ died for our sins, established a kingdom for us, made us heirs with him of all the riches of the kingdom, and is on hand to usher us into the joys of that kingdom. The remorse, the regrets, the guilt of the past can all be put away, and we can plunge into the riches of God's grace with nothing holding us back. The Holy Spirit is not a killjoy. His call is to a life of glory.

I believe that Christ died for my sins. Is that faith?

Yes, it is faith. But it may be a kind of dead, intellectual faith. If you say, "I believe the world is round," that's a kind of faith, too. But your life goes on the same whether you believe the world is round or flat.

Faith in Christ goes beyond accepting the truth of certain facts. It means to trust him, really count on him. And when you have faith, you want to thank Christ by obeying him. Real faith is an active sort of thing (see James 2:26). To believe—to have faith—in Christ as your Lord and Savior makes a world of difference in your life. That's the kind of faith the Holy Spirit is at work to give you.

How does the Holy Spirit do his work?

He works primarily through the Word and the sacraments. This may sound a bit strange and limiting. But if you read and hear God's Word with a sincere intention of listening and doing what he wants you to do, you will know that his Word has strange power. The Bible is not like any other book. The Holy Spirit is in those pages and he intends to have Christ leap from the pages and enter your heart (see Hebrews 4:12). And when you go to the Lord's Supper, even if you don't feel any special sadness or gladness, be sure of this: the Holy Spirit is there to give you blessings in rich measure.

For reflection

1. Read 1 Samuel 3:9-18 for the story of Samuel listening to God. Read Acts 9:1-9 for the story of Paul listening to God.

2. Recall a time when you heard God's Spirit speaking to you.

3. How can you take time to listen for God's voice?

21

United in Christ

The Third Article

The Holy Spirit brings us to Christ, not only to him but into him, and he brings Christ not only to us but into us. Of all the imagery the Bible uses to describe the work of the Holy Spirit, this highly personalized picture is the most profound.

Words and pictures are obviously limited in what they can do. We are dealing with a deep and wonderful mystery—how God and people can be united, and what happens when they are. Words can carry some cargo, but the divine and eternal are too full and vast for the best of human vehicles. As Paul said, we see in a mirror dimly. But God is gracious; he takes these human vehicles, words and pictures and water and wine and bread, and comes to us in and through them.

The Holy Spirit is the announcer calling us to a new life waiting for us. He is an usher, prodding and directing us into the kingdom. He is the tree surgeon, grafting us as branches into the trunk which is Christ. He is the instructor, enlightening our hearts and minds. He is a fire burning out the dross in us. He is above all and foremost the guide, leading us to Christ.

We have spoken of Christ as the warrior who wins the war and gives us the victory; we have seen him as the judge and Savior, who forgives our sins; we have called him our companion and brother and the Lord who befriends us and rules us. We worship him as God, God the Son, as head of the body, the church.

Whatever description we use, each is a key to his love for us. Now, in going a step further, we say that he is in us and we are in him. We are one with him, yet not one. He is still high and lifted up at God's right hand, and we join the great throng who adore him and praise him and thank him. But he is in us, and we are in him.

And he who is all in all, God and man, lifts us with him into a life which makes all things new. He affects everything we do. It is the same life we have always lived—we eat, we sleep, we work, we marry, we get sick, and we die. But all of this (our common life) now is transferred out of the kingdom of this world into his glorious kingdom. The whole drama of life has been shifted to a new setting, to a new stage, with a new director.

This may sound like so much unintelligible talk, a sort of mysticism, some strange dream. How can two people be one? The Bible, however, is full of this sort of language in speaking about Christ and his own.

In our human experience, of course, no two people have been fused into one. No matter how much two people love one another, they will, like two pebbles on the beach, remain two. They may be tumbled together by the surf, polishing one another, shaping one another, but they will not finally be merged into one.

But the Bible is not talking here about two people; it is talking about God and you, or God and me. In Christ we can be one with God, for he is God. We do not achieve this by strange or endless disciplines of meditation. The Holy Spirit brings this about by grace through faith. It is a gift.

The same language is used of the church. The church is the bride of Christ (Ephesians 5:23-27). This is the nearest human parallel to the reality being expressed: ". . . and they shall be one flesh." The church is the body of Christ, he the head and we the organs and cells—one body (Romans 12:4-5).

If we are in Christ, "hidden in Christ," then we have all the gifts which Christ gives. And what a galaxy that is: love, forgiveness, hope, courage, peace, patience, kindness. They are like seeds, planted at Baptism when the life of Christ was given, waiting to grow and blossom.

Being the kind of person I am, how dare I presume to have Christ in me?

The level of your worthiness or unworthiness has nothing to do with the *fact* that at Baptism Christ took up residence in you. You would never dare to invite him or have him if you first were to prepare a "house" befitting him. Remember, he came into a very messy world, became a part of it, and set himself to the task of redeeming it (see Matthew 9:12). You are that world, or a part of it.

If I live in him and he lives in me, do I get involved in doing everything he does?

In a sense, yes. You are crucified with him, and you are raised to a newness of life with him. This is both a once-and-for-all event and an ongoing process. The old Adam in you—your sinful inclinations—is daily drowned and buried, as Luther said, and the new person Christ has created in you daily rises to a life in and with Christ. Moreover, you are now deeply involved in his suffering for the sake of others, in his warfare against all evil, and best of all, in his glory (see Philippians 1:20-21).

Christ is the ruler of all. Do I share in his rulership?

Indeed you do. He makes you lord of all. You are an heir in his kingdom. You are no slave or common laborer (see 1 Peter 2:9). But—and here's the rub—like him, you who are lord of all now become the servant and slave of all. His lordship is a reversal of all other sovereignties. He uses his power in love to let all people have a claim on him. And his pattern of rulership now becomes yours.

Can I lose him?

He will not leave you, but you can leave him. Some do. If you do, you surrender a kingdom, you abandon this new world of love and forgiveness, you slip back into a flat world of humdrum and boredom where you eat, sleep, marry, and die with no high commission and no soaring hope. It would be a sorry exchange.

Am I likely to be more Christ-like at the age of sixty than at the age of twenty?

When you are sixty, you yourself may not be able to say with any confidence that you are now more Christ-like than you were at the age of twenty. The best evidence of your growth may be an increasing awareness that you need God's help. But the Holy Spirit surely intends that you grow in those qualities that are Christ-like. And if we put ourselves in his path (through the Word and sacrament, prayer, fellowship with other believers, deeds of love and mercy), we should have confidence that his work in us is indeed meeting with some success. But only God can measure. And Satan is hard at work to stop any growth.

Are people who are in Christ tempted more than those who are not?

Most likely they are. To be in Christ is to be lined up on his battlefield with him, and the enemy will use all his wiles to have such a soldier defect and leave the field—to give up on something he knows to be God's will, for instance, for personal profit or because of pressure from friends. But if we remain in him who has overcome the world, then we too shall overcome.

For reflection

1. Read Romans 6:3-4, Galatians 2:20, and Colossians 3:3-34, and ask yourself what it means for you to be in Christ.

2. Christ is in you. When you stop to think about that fact, what difference does it make? How does it affect the way you live?

22

This Mysterious Body

The Third Article

It's Sunday, and I'm in church. I take a look around to see who's here. I spot many of my friends as well as a few strangers. The pastor is here; the organist and choir are here.

The Lord is here! He has promised to be where two or three are gathered in his name. Who else is here? It occurs to me that if we are the body of Christ, then wherever Christ is, there everyone who belongs to him must in some strange and wonderful way be there too. My children and grandchildren must be here; they belong to him. How about my grandparents? They are long since gone from this earth. But they died believing in Christ and are with him. Since Christ is here, they must be here too.

Hold it! Isn't my imagination now running ahead of the truth? Have I a right to marshal all these people into this hour and this place? I think I do. I think I must. This mysterious body called the church, the church on earth and the church in heaven, is one glorious company in the Lord. And whenever any part of it is gathered, the whole of it must in some way be there.

Abraham and Sarah and Paul and Peter and St. Francis and Luther and Mother Theresa and Bonhoeffer are here. The church in India and the church in Africa are here. So, we lift our voices and say, "Therefore, with angels and archangels and all the company of heaven, we laud and magnify thy glorious name."

The one holy Christian and apostolic church on earth and in heaven is here. We cannot divide the body of Christ, nor can we sort it out into fragments.

But isn't this congregation something different? It has officers and budgets. It is a legal corporation, registered as such in the courthouse. Isn't it more like the International Red Cross or a business?

It is like that, to be sure, but it is also much different. It is more like a living cell in a living body. It is the body of Christ, the communion of saints, with no other organization than allegiance to its one head, Jesus Christ. And when the congregation gathers to pray and praise around the Word and the sacraments, then it is not a meeting of the corporation, but rather a celebration of the great, eternal family.

While Christ alone knows who are truly members of his body and mot merely pretenders, we must believe that within the congregations the Holy Spirit has brought and kept many people in the living faith. When we write the history of the Christian church, therefore, we tell the story of congregations and of church denominations.

The history of the church is a most impressive history. It began on the day of Pentecost in Jerusalem some two thousand years ago, when the Holy Spirit came in wind and fire to a group in an upper room. Think what that first, small band of followers did in the very first century, fanning out into all the nations on the Mediterranean. In the succeeding years the church spread from there across oceans into all the world, until today it is found in all nations the world over. They came with the story of Jesus, Lord and Savior, and the story captured hundreds of millions.

They came with more than a story. They came with the witness of a new life. The world looked at them and said, "See how they love one another." Into this cold and indifferent world came a new and radical love, the love of God in Jesus Christ.

In the centuries that have followed, the Christian church has started almost every existing institution for the care of the poor, the needy, the sick, and the homeless. Also, almost all the schools were begun as schools of the church.

The church has some dark chapters, when it forgot or refused to follow its Lord, but they cannot match or annul the measureless good that God has been able to channel in and through the church. We need never be ashamed to claim membership in the church.

The church on earth is called "militant" because it fights against evil in the world and in itself. The church in heaven is called "triumphant" because there the saved are raised from death to live with their Lord in glory and victory forever. And this church, in earth and heaven, is one!

Is the holy Christian church the same as all the denominations put together?

No, not quite the same. The holy Christian church is a reality in itself. It is found in all the denominations that confess Jesus as Lord, but it is not the same as a collection of congregations or denominations. You may have been baptized *in* a Lutheran church, but you were baptized *into* the holy Christian church.

How important is it to be in the church?

To be a true member of the church of Jesus Christ is to belong to him, and belonging to him is the most important thing in your life. Any other "belonging" that you have—in a family, in a country—will someday end. Only God's family is forever.

Can I belong to the holy Christian church without belonging to one of the congregations or denominations?

Probably, but it would seem strange. This would mean that you want to belong to Christ but not to any organization that bears his name. This would be as if you want to be a citizen of the United States, but not of any of the 50 states. You would also be denying yourself the strength that comes through the sacraments and Christian fellowship (see Hebrews 10:25).

Is it all right to criticize the church?

If it seems right for you to criticize yourself, then it's probably right for you to criticize your church (your congregation or your denomination). When you do, be sure to say *my* church, and not *the* church, because you are as much the church as the pastor or the choir. Christ regards you as such.

How important is it to attend worship regularly?

More important than you may think. This is your weekly appointment to gather with the Lord's family to thank and praise him and learn from him. Use the imagination God has given you; think what a privilege it is to come into the presence of God and be in the great company of the one church.

Does the church keep changing from age to age?

In many ways. It has to meet the needs of people in every age, and these needs change. But perhaps the church changes less than most things. It has the same gospel, the same great message the apostles had. It often uses the same hymns that our great grandparents sang. Though it should be responsive to new gifts that the Holy Spirit wants to give to enrich the church, there is still something exhilarating about worshiping with some of the old liturgies and songs which generations have used before us. The Lord is the same yesterday, today, and forever, and his church in a very deep sense is the same too (Hebrews 13:8).

How can I help my church be a better church?

You start with yourself. If you are faithful in attendance, if you support your church, if you set out to be a friend to people, if in your private life you pray and meditate on God's Word, and if as a citizen you seek to do God's will in your work, your home, and your community, you will by your example give support to others who are in the church. Doors will open so that you who are in Christ will bring the strength and comfort of Christ to others.

For reflection

1. Read Christ's "high priestly prayer" in John 17, especially verses 20-26, which is both a description of his church and his prayer for it, and consider that he means to include you.

2. How does the church of Christ connect the past, present, and future?

3. What is most important to you about being part of Christ's body, the church?

23

Fruits and Gifts

The Third Article

Once the Holy Spirit has us ushered into Christ and his kingdom, he goes on to give us gifts and nourishes us so that we bear fruit.

Of fruit the apostle Paul says, "The fruit of the Spirit is love, joy, peace, patience, kindness, goodness, faithfulness, gentleness, self-control" (Galatians 5:22-23). And he adds, "Against such there is no law." In other words, all people will agree that these qualities are desirable in everyone.

It is a bit different with gifts of the Spirit. In 1 Corinthians 12-14 the apostle discusses the variety of capacities or gifts that the Spirit gives within the church. He implies that one kind of gift may be given to one person and another kind may be given to another person. It is like a large service station and repair shop, where each worker has a different skill and each skill is of importance for the good operation of the shop. One may be an expert in wheels, another in transmissions, another in electrical work, another in keeping books, another at waiting on customers.

In the church it is not necessary that everyone have the same gift nor that anyone have all the gifts of the Spirit. None of us should conclude, therefore, that because we have one gift and not another we are of little or no importance to the life of the church.

In our life in Christ the one, towering gift or fruit is love. Paul spends an entire chapter on this one gift (1 Corinthians 13), and elevates it far above all others. It is love that swallows up all the differences and makes us one. The shortest definition of God is, "God is love."

Think how God must like differences or variety. No two snowflakes are alike nor any two people. He made each of us different from everyone else in the world. There is only one you. There will never be another.

Of all the gifts which Paul names, the most puzzling are these four: the working of miracles, the gifts of healing, the gift of tongues, and the interpretation of tongues. They are difficult to understand because they appear only occasionally.

The early disciples performed miracles, chiefly of healing. Also, in the early church there were people who spoke in "tongues," a language of praise which was different from any other standard language and could be translated into understandable words only by someone who had the special gift of interpretation.

Perhaps the Holy Spirit knew that the young church had need of these added reassurances that God was in their midst. And now when the church has grown in strength, perhaps the Holy Spirit reduces or withholds these gifts for fear that they may distract the church from the greater gifts of faith, hope, and love.

In recent years, however, a new interest in these special gifts has grown, especially in tongues and healing. Those who do get these gifts must always remember that they are minor or lesser gifts, not to be compared with the impressive fruits of the Spirit that all people may have and should have.

After all, are not all good gifts from God? Isn't the vast medical knowledge that he has given to doctors an extension of the few special healings in the early church? And isn't the gift of speech itself a marvelous miracle? You have ideas in your brain that move muscles in your lungs, throat, tongue, and lips to produce words. The words become sound waves, strike your friends' eardrums, and these become translated into ideas in their brains. To Paul, too, this was the greater wonder: "I would rather speak five words with my mind, in order to instruct others, than ten thousand words in a tongue" (1 Corinthians 14:19).

But let us not forget that God has made us different, and has sorted out different gifts. If and when some people have had a different experience with God than you have had, do not become uneasy. If we always remember that we are made one in Christ to love him and one another, the differences can enrich the church.

Should I pray for these special gifts?

Paul said we should earnestly desire these gifts. Yet to be so eager to have the gift of tongues, for instance, that your mind actually covets this gift and your time is spent in pursuit of it, may distract you from desiring and praying for other rich fruits of the Spirit.

Can I make these fruits grow?

No more than a farmer can make his wheat grow. He puts the seed (which he doesn't make) into the ground (which he doesn't make either), and waits for the sunshine and the rain. He must, of course, clear the field of weeds and be at work to fight off insects and rust. But he doesn't ripen the grain (see 1 Corinthians 3:6).

In this matter of growing in grace, you don't just sit and wait. You attend to the Word and the sacraments, you pray, you do deeds of love. But all of this is in response to God's action. The love and joy and peace that grow in your heart will always be the Spirit's work in you.

Can we block the Spirit from doing his work with us?

In many ways, such as neglecting Bible reading, prayer, and worship, avoiding the fellowship of other Christians, or failing to do what we know God wants us to do. He is always ready to do much more for us and in us than we dare to ask, or sometimes dare to let him (Ephesians 3:20).

If I get sick and the doctors don't seem to make me well, should I seek out someone who has the gift of healing?

Some people do and some people don't. It certainly would not be wrong to do so—if you remember two things. First, it is God who has given doctors also "the gift of healing," through the amazing knowledge given to them. It would be wrong to bypass these gifts that God has given, by failing to make use of available scientific medicine. Second, remember that God has not promised that everyone will get well, whether through medicine or other means, such as a special healing service. If you don't get well, it would be wrong to conclude that God is against you or that you have too little faith to move him.

We believe that God hears the prayers for healing offered by any Christian, not only those of some special "healer." By all means let us pray for healing; God himself has urged us to do so.

Sometimes I wish God would show his hand in some special way, like a miracle.

Almost everyone wishes that. But most of us will have to trust him, that he is doing many wonderful things for us, day by day, in ways that we cannot see or understand or measure. There may be moments when he seems especially near, or instances when our prayers clearly have been answered. But he has given us the great gift of faith to trust him even when nothing exciting seems to happen. The quiet, steady growth of faith, hope, and love in our hearts is indeed a miracle.

For reflection

1. Read 1 John 4:13-21 to learn how we can tell that the Spirit is at work in us.

2. What particular gifts do you feel God has given you?

24

Turning the Page

The Third Article

When death is done with us, what then? Is that the end? Are we like the flame of a candle blown out, and that's all? Or is our life here only the first chapter, and we turn the page to go on and on?

In the Apostles' Creed we end with these sweeping words, "I believe . . . in the resurrection of the body and the life everlasting." Death was not the end for Jesus, and it is not the end for us.

Long ago people thought that this earth was all there is to the universe, and above the world was stretched a canopy, like an umbrella. During the day there was one bright light, the sun, and at night the moon and the stars. Up above the canopy somewhere was heaven, where all of Christ's followers would gather after death.

Today we live in an age of space travel. We have set foot on the moon and launched numerous unmanned vehicles a billion miles out into the universe. We now know that out there, far beyond our solar system, are myriad suns, planets, and galaxies, billions of light years away.

Somewhere in God's wonderful kingdom he has a place for us after death. It's not a weird, ghostly place where, like wisps of vapor or bits of fog, we drift around. It is a place for bodies like yours and mine, except now glorified, more real by far than the bodies we now have. Nor will these bodies ever wear out or have pain. And we shall live with God, with his angels, and with each other forever. Could anything be more exciting than this?

The world is an exciting place too. Most of us do not want to leave it. In spite of all its troubles, it is our home at the moment and we are in no great hurry to move on. And it, too, is God's world, a part of his empire, and he has put us to work here. He doesn't want us to resign.

It would be a pity, however, if we thought this world were good enough. With all its wars and crimes and hunger and disease, it's not good enough. In the same way, you and I, too, even at our best, are not good enough. Deep down, we ought to long for another place in God's empire where life will be the kind that God wants for his children. He has promised that there is such a place waiting for us.

Almost all people the world over, from the dawn of history, have had some notion of life after death. It was the resurrection of Jesus that turned this notion into a flaming faith for those who believe in him. He said, "I go to prepare a place for you."

No one has returned from this part of God's empire to tell us precisely how things are there. But we have the promise of our Lord that there is a house waiting for us. We count on this promise, without having a preview. Jesus discussed the question in a parable whether someone could not be dispatched from the dead to tell people about the afterlife (Luke 16:19-31). The answer was that if people refused to believe the promises of Scripture, they wouldn't accept the report of someone coming back from the dead either. Jesus himself did come back, and our trust is in him.

Moreover, heaven is so wonderful that we probably couldn't stand even a glimpse or preview. Our earthly eyes and minds would be shattered by the sheer glory of it.

It is of tremendous comfort to think that our dear ones, those who have died in the Lord, are there with their Lord, serving and enjoying him forever.

Charlie, only thirteen, was a great guy and a follower of Jesus. He was killed in an accident. Is he now in heaven?

Of course. That's what Jesus promised.

But doesn't the resurrection of the body occur on the last day, when the Lord returns in glory?

This is one of the pictures of Scripture (John 5:28-29). It implies that until Christ returns we shall be "asleep in Jesus," awaiting the great day. Another scene (Hebrews 12:1) pictures those who have gone on to be with the Lord as if they are now in a great stadium, surrounding and perhaps cheering us who are still on the track, running the race of life.

Why be troubled about just *how* we shall be with Jesus? The great fact is that we shall be with him. Also, time and space may not be quite the same in that part of the empire. Most people find comfort in the thought that at once, when death can do no more, the Lord raises us up to live in conscious joy with him.

Does Jesus give us any clue about what kind of body we will have?

Yes. Like his resurrected body, it will be "glorified." It will be a real body, but in a more wonderful condition than the one we now have. Sin and its effects will be removed. Death cannot touch the body anymore. Remember what Jesus was like when he lived with his followers those forty days after his resurrection and before his ascension. This is the clue (see 1 Corinthians 15:42-44).

What about the soul? Is that anything different from the body?

We do talk about body and soul as if we are made up of two parts. It may be better, even more scriptural, to think of "soul" as meaning the real you—mind, spirit, body, soul—all together. God created the whole you, and he wants the whole you restored to him in heaven.

Why do people take such good care of cemeteries or graveyards?

Perhaps because of memories. It is the spot where the old body has been laid to rest, and memories naturally cluster around that place. For believers it is more than a memory; it is a reminder that their dear ones are not doomed only to be reabsorbed into the soil, but that there will be a resurrection and new bodies. Cemeteries need not be melancholy places. They can be quiet reminders of the Lord's great promises.

What about hell?

It is difficult to think of a merciful God sentencing someone to hell. The Bible does indicate that there are people who separate themselves from God during their life in such a way that God cannot reach them and save them. In a deep sense, God does not send anyone to hell. People send themselves by not wanting anything to with God.

Will heaven be different from the life we have here?

Yes and no. Unhappiness, pain, and death will be gone, and that will be different. Everything will be good and right. But just as we have our Lord here, through faith, we shall have him there, by sight (Revelation 21:3-4). It could well be that God will have in his heavens many of the things we have found good here. When a boy asked his mother if his dog, Tikki, would be in heaven, she said, "I'm quite sure he will." We don't know, of course. But if Tikki will be necessary for this boy's joy in heaven, Tikki will be there. There will be nothing to diminish our joy!

For reflection

1. Read 1 Corinthians 15:12-26 for assurance that he who raised Christ from the dead will raise us also.

2. How can the promise of new lives after death help us in our lives in the present?

3. What do you imagine heaven to be like?

The Lord's Prayer

25

An Invitation to Talk

You would think that an executive who owns and runs a business of billions of worlds and galaxies would try to get some privacy. But not our Lord. He has given every person on earth not only the right but the invitation to dial him directly at any time. And there'll never be a busy signal.

It is in prayer that our life with God becomes fascinating, comforting, and sometimes disturbing. The moment we accept his invitation to pray we really give him an invitation to enter our lives. If we want to keep him at arm's length, we had better not start talking to him. Many people don't.

Of course, if we take seriously the idea that he is our heavenly Father, it would be strange if we didn't talk with him when he has invited us to do so—unless, of course, we're afraid to.

And from one point of view there is good reason to fear. Give God an inch and he may take a mile. Call him in for a small repair job, and he may set out to remodel the whole house. Your life may never be the same again.

God has promised, "Ask and you will receive." But it may be that you will receive something different, something much more, than you have ever asked. You're just looking for a part-time job, and God makes you vice-president of the firm.

Yet considering the possible benefits in store for us, we would be foolish not to take the risk that we'll get more than we bargained for. God respects every kind of prayer, even the trivial and silly kind. Like any good father, he would much rather that you came with any small matter than that you never came at all. You honor him by coming, by counting on him. He will sort out your prayers, recognizing that some are more significant than others. God may even chuckle over some of them. But God takes you seriously and will never cut you off.

Prayer is more like talking things over with a friend than like telephoning an order to the grocer. You pour out your troubles, your fears, your hopes, your joys, laying them out in the presence of God. And God does not just silently listen. He responds. He speaks to us in his Word, he stirs our minds and consciences to find and do his will, he takes us by the hand and leads us through doors that open to great blessings.

It gives us confidence to know that Jesus Christ has repaired the connections that once were cut. We were alienated from God, had become enemies of his, and faced him only as lawbreakers before a judge. But Christ died on a cross to change all that, so that in forgiveness and faith we find the channel to God wide open again. We now can come to him to be helped and corrected, not to be condemned and sentenced. We come not as enemies and strangers, but as sons and daughters. Nor do we come to demand our rewards, but to receive his gifts.

We can trust God to want for us only that which is good. Anything evil that happens to us is not of God. We thank him for all good; we blame him for nothing bad. To be sure, we do not always know what is good for us, but we pray for what we think is good and trust him to deliver only that which really is good.

God is especially pleased to have us pray for others. The very climate of his kingdom leads us to do this. We have been shifted from self-concern, self-defense, and self-pity to the care of one another. It is not strange in the kingdom for a person to defend the rights of others more than his own rights, to feel the hurts and fears of his friend more deeply than his own. The poor, the oppressed, the lonely, the discouraged—these become the burden of our prayers.

We do not need to form complete sentences when we pray. God is not a grammarian. We can pray without words at all. He hears the faintest sigh. Our very thoughts, directed to God, become prayers. In fact, the very posture of our lives may be facing him, so that even when we are too busy to think of him or talk to him we are still in communication with him.

Do we change God's mind by praying?

From a number of instances in Scripture, it would seem so (Exodus 32:10-14; 2 Kings 20:1-6). You don't make him love you more by praying, but within that great love of his it does seem possible that prayer effects changes. It would be ridiculous, even cruel, for him to urge that we pray if our prayers were futile. We cannot know the workings of the mind of God, however, so let us simply say that God changes things instead of saying that God changes his mind.

Is it possible that the only change is in us who pray, and that through us other changes come about?

It would hardly seem that God's control of his universe is limited only to the changes he can effect in us. We cannot control or manipulate God, but neither can we restrict God's freedom and power.

Won't God do what's good for us without our asking?

Yes, but he has invited us to ask. Of course prayer is not only asking for something. The significance of prayer is that we can thereby communicate with God, regardless of what happens. Wouldn't it be strange if the only time a son and daughter talked with their father and mother was when they wanted something? The finest talks they have together are very likely those occasions when no one asks anything. They simply enjoy one another and talk things over. In its highest form, prayer may be just that.

He has told us to pray for specific things, hasn't he?

Yes, largely for other people—for all who are in need, for those who minister the gospel, for leaders in government and society (1 Timothy 2:1-2). Also he has told us to pray that the world might have peace and that God's will be done.

Has he not told us to pray for healing?

Yes, and we all do. In fact, since most people do get sick at one time or another, this is one of the most common prayers. Some churches have special services where prayers for healing are specifically encouraged. It may be questioned whether prayers for health should be in any different class from prayers for good weather, safety in travel, or peace among nations. And certainly, more important than any of these would be prayers for forgiveness and for growth in Christ-likeness.

What part does the Holy Spirit play in our prayers?

The Scriptures assure us that the Holy Spirit will help us pray as we ought to pray, and will intercede for us (Romans 8:26).

Does the Holy Spirit give us a special language for prayer?

Occasionally some person may get the gift of tongues, which appears to be a language of praise. Since this is unintelligible (except to God or to someone with the gift of interpretation) and may even sound like gibberish, the Scriptures counsel that this language should be used privately and not in the company of other people. It should not be implied that people without this gift cannot praise God adequately.

Should a person have stated times for prayer?

This is highly advisable, since we can so easily be distracted from praying at all. To thank God in the morning, to pray his blessings upon our meals, to put ourselves in his care as we go to sleep—these are natural occasions. Certainly to gather with fellow Christians on Sunday for prayer, praise, and thanksgiving is a privilege that should be gladly observed.

For reflection

1. Read Philippians 4:4-7 for guidance on how to pray and for insight as to what prayer's greatest reward will be.

2. When do you pray? Have you set aside a special time for prayer?

3. Finish this phrase: For me, prayer is _____.

26

When You Pray the Lord's Prayer

Jesus often went off by himself to pray. One day the disciples asked him to teach them how to pray. He then gave them what has since been known as the Lord's Prayer. It is the one prayer that is prayed by Christians the world over.

Most of us know this prayer so well that our tongues will say the words while our thoughts wander, and we may actually not be praying at all. We need to discipline our minds to know and remember what we are asking. Let us take a look at each of the seven petitions of this prayer.

The prayer opens with a simple address: "Our Father who art in heaven." It is a great privilege that I can come to him as his child. God is not a king on a throne or an executive in an inner office; he is the Father of my Lord and my Father who loves me more than any earthly father or mother can ever love.

And in saying *our* Father, I am reminded that I am a member of God's family, the church, and that we all pray with and for one another. God is really the Father of all the people on earth, and he wants us to claim one another as brothers and sisters in his great family.

I pray "Hallowed be thy name," and remember that God's name is held in reverence by us only as his Word is taught in its truth and purity, when we believe it, and when our lives are such that people can see that we love and obey them.

"Thy kingdom come." Ever since Christ was raised from the dead, the kingdom is in our midst. We pray here that the Holy Spirit may secure the kingdom in our hearts, that we may be within the kingdom and have peace and joy in the Holy Spirit. We also ask that more people be included in God's church.

"Thy will be done, on earth as it is in heaven." The powers of evil are great, both within us and in the world. They are pitted against God's will being done. We pray God to defeat these foes within us and in the world, so that we may be and have what he wants for us.

"Give us this day our daily bread." I find this prayer the easiest to pray, because I naturally want food and shelter, a happy family, a good government, friends, and world peace. All of these and more are in the catalog of my wants and needs. The word *daily* cautions me against worrying about the future, and reminds me to be content with what the Lord provides.

"Forgive us our trespasses, as we forgive those who trespass against us." In one sense this is the most important prayer of all. Sin is like a wall separating us from God and from one another, and forgiveness shatters that wall. Now, forgiven of God, I pray for the grace to forgive others and to be forgiven of others.

"Lead us not into temptation." Since God is not the tempter, we pray that he will keep us from being tempted by evil or from being crushed by disaster—and that when we are tested by such adversities, we may be given strength to resist and to overcome.

"But deliver us from evil." We have been delivered from the dominion or tyranny of the evil powers by Christ's victory, but "the devil, the world, and our sinful self" still trouble us and seek to capture us. As people who have been set free by Christ, we pray for his help to be faithful warriors against all shapes of evil.

The church has added a doxology, "For thine is the kingdom, the power, and the glory, for ever and ever. Amen." This reminds us that our Father can indeed answer these prayers and that he will, and we thank him for hearing us.

As we pray this prayer in a church service, we may hardly have time to ponder the full meaning of each petition. But when we pray it alone, as we should each day, it is a good habit to pause between each sentence to dwell on what we are actually asking of God.

If a prayer becomes too familiar, isn't it better to pray it in your own words?

It's not a question of either/or. Certainly Christians should pour out their hearts to God in their own words. But old prayers which the church has used for centuries bind us together across the years. Moreover, many such prayers have the marks of the Holy Spirit's guiding us all in what is most important to pray for.

The Lord's Prayer, repetitious as it becomes, is in a class by itself. It is the one prayer the Lord himself taught us to pray. It would be impossible to think of replacing it with a prayer of our own making. We pray in the words of the Lord's Prayer, in the words of other great and old prayers, and in our own words.

If God is the Father of all people everywhere, is this prayer for the Christian church alone?

God in his love is responsive to the needs of all his creatures. But only as Christ has revealed God to us as a loving Father, and only as we have been reconciled to God through the work of Christ for us—only then will we have the faith to know God as our Father and have the confidence and courage to come to him as his beloved children. Without this revelation and reconciliation, God will always seem unknown and far off (see Galatians 4:6-7).

Are not all seven petitions things that God wants to do for us anyway? Why bother God repeatedly with this prayer?

Yes, all seven are certainly within God's will. But Jesus did tell us to pray for these, and Jesus is our Lord. So we obey and pray. We also pray that we may be included in these intentions of God for his people.

There are no intercessions in this prayer, are there?

Not explicitly. But in praying for the coming of the kingdom and for God's will to be done on earth, we are asking for his blessings upon the whole world, not alone for ourselves and for the Christian church.

In most of our prayers we add, "In Jesus' name" or "For the sake of Jesus." Why not here?

Jesus did tell us to pray to the Father in his name (John 14:13). But those exact words need not always be used. In the Lord's Prayer, as in any prayer, we approach God with confidence only through the merits and intercession of Jesus, our brother and Savior.

Is God more likely to give daily bread to those who pray for it?

No. God is impartial in his love and he makes provision for our elemental needs whether we pray or not, or whether we have come to him or not. He "sends rain on the just and on the unjust" (Matthew 5:45). We who see God as the giver will have greater joy in his gifts than those who forget that there is a giver (see Psalm 145:15-16).

Is adversity or disaster less likely to happen to those who pray to be delivered from evil?

Maybe. People who pray for God's guidance and protection are less likely to do things that bring unhappiness into their lives. They may be kept from drunkenness, infidelity, dishonesty—things which bring pain and suffering. But prayer will not necessarily deflect a tornado from its path nor stop a river from flooding your house.

For reflection

1. Read Matthew 6:7-15 and Luke 11:1-4 for the accounts of the disciples receiving the Lord's Prayer and think of how we use it today.

2. How might you pray the Lord's Prayer in a way that makes it more meaningful for you?

3. How does this one prayer summarize much of the Christian faith?

The Sacraments

27

What Happens at Baptism?

At birth we are born into a life on earth; at Baptism we are born into a life in the kingdom of God. In neither birth do we take the initiative. Both are gifts from God.

It is a mark of obedience that we practice Baptism. And obedience itself is important. The last command Jesus gave his disciples was, "Go therefore and make disciples of all nations, baptizing them" (Matthew 28:19).

What precisely happens when a person is baptized? Let us examine some of the answers. Whatever answer we give, there still remains the mystery of God's loving way with people.

Baptism means that now the person is a member of the congregation. And of course, a member of more than the congregation. Every person is baptized into the holy Christian church, the body of Christ on earth, whether he or she is baptized in the Lutheran church, the Presbyterian church, the Catholic church, or any other Christian church.

We also speak of the person being grafted into Christ through Baptism, as a branch is grafted into the trunk of the tree. This image comes from the way Christ described himself as the vine and us as branches (John 15:1-5).

Baptism is also called the washing of regeneration (Titus 3:5), which means it is a new beginning, a new birth. By our own will or efforts, none of us can have this new life. Christ enters, takes away our sinfulness, and brings his life into our hearts.

We even speak of the gift of faith being given in Baptism. Whether faith is given when a person is grown and is aware of having faith, or whether it is given to a baby, faith always remains a pure gift from God.

All of these answers put together are not enough. The wonder is that by the simple use of water, coupled with God's promises, God's life is brought to us.

The fact that a child cannot yet know about these blessings need not bother us. Suppose a child has a rich uncle who, hearing that he has a niece, deposits $100,000 into the child's account in the bank. It will be several years before the child can possibly know what $100,000 is like. But by the act of the uncle, the child has become rich. By the action of God in Baptism, the child is offered a kingdom, and her parents and sponsors accept it for her.

Until a person dies, his Christian faith will be anchored in his Baptism, flow out from it, return to it, and blossom in it. In Martin Luther's solitary struggles for peace of soul, when the devil tempted him to doubt and despair, he once carved these words on the table, *"Baptizatus sum!"* (I am baptized!). Nothing can change that. Once and for all, in the Sacrament of Holy Baptism, God has claimed you.

This is not merely a nice practice of the church, but a sacrament. A sacrament is a holy act, instituted by God, in which by visible means be bestows and seals his invisible grace. It is an act of adoption. We are made children of God.

Why is Baptism sometimes called a covenant?

A covenant is a commitment or pledge or promise. In Baptism God promises to forgive us our sin, give us eternal life, and make us his children. In response, we renounce the devil and all his works and declare our belief in God.

What does it mean to renounce the devil and all his works and all his ways?

It means that a person faces the fact of evil, acknowledges its reality and its strength, and now in the power of God renounces it. In a sense, a person is born in the devil's prison, and at Baptism is asked if he or she will leave that prison and its way of life and will fight against evil in all its forms.

What does it mean to believe in God, the Father, Son, and Holy Spirit?

It means to embrace the faith of the church. This means that although we recognize our failings, we entrust ourselves to God for forgiveness because of what Christ has done, and for guidance in a life of gratitude and obedience, now and forever.

How can parents, sponsors, and the congregation have made these commitments for me and others baptized as infants?

As a little child you could hardly have made them for yourself. So the church wisely appointed the people to whom you naturally "belong," your parents and Christian sponsors, to make the renunciation and confession for you.

Let's try an example. Suppose you were born in the United States. When you were one year old, your folks emigrated to Australia to be citizens there, and took you with them. Later, when you are grown, you would indicate for yourself whether you wanted to claim the citizenship committed to you by your parents.

Your parents and sponsors have committed you to Christ's church in Holy Baptism. As you grow older you make the confession for yourself, in the Sunday services, at the time of your confirmation, and at other times.

If we turn against God, then what?

God never breaks his covenant with us. If we leave him he waits for us to come back, like the father in the story of the prodigal son, and he is overjoyed to have us return. You never have to be baptized over again; you need only to return to the covenant still held out to you by God (see 2 Timothy 2:13).

Does anyone ever remain in this covenant relationship all of his life, and never fall away?

Yes. In fact, that ought to be the normal way for all of us. If we hear his Word and come to the Lord's Supper with regularity, and if we pray and try to do our Lord's will, it would seem strange for us to fall away. This does not mean that we will be perfect or that we will always obey him.

If I have doubts, and if I don't feel excited about God, does that mean that I have fallen away?

Not necessarily. You may always have some doubts. In fact, it is sometimes easiest to doubt that which means most to us. This was probably the case with Thomas after Christ's resurrection. Also, remember that you can't always control your feelings. Sometimes you're up and sometimes you're down. We are to trust God's Word, his promises, firmly fastened to our baptismal covenant.

If a child has not been baptized and dies, is that child lost to God?

Neither the Lord nor the church has ever made that restriction. Our Lord is a most merciful Lord, and we must trust God to care for the unbaptized child.

Why is water used?

Because Jesus told us to use water. The ancient philosophers considered water the basic element of the world, and as such it stands for the whole of matter. It is also the natural symbol of life, for there is no life without water. In Baptism it is also a symbol of death—the drowning of the old Adam, that is, our sinful nature. And it is a symbol of purification, for there is no cleanliness without it. In the sacrament, water becomes a vehicle of God's grace.

Do parents and sponsors make any commitments for themselves?

They promise to help the child grow up in the faith by praying for him, by loving him, by teaching him about God, by bringing him to church, and by encouraging him to live a Christian life. The congregation, too, has a responsibility to provide opportunities for Christian nurture.

For reflection

1. Read Romans 6:1-11 and Galatians 3:23-28 to learn how central this sacrament was in the life of the early church.

2. What does God promise to give us in Baptism?

3. Someone has described Christian living as "walking wet." What do you think that means?

28

Together at Supper

The Lord's Supper

It was Thursday evening. The next day Jesus would die. He knew it and he told his disciples. They were at supper together, a farewell meal.

As they had come into the room, Jesus had taken a basin of water and a towel and had washed the dusty feet of each one. Normally this chore was done only by some lowly servant. Jesus did it to remind them that they should never be too proud to serve one another.

As they were seated around the table, he took bread and wine and told them that this was his body and blood and that they should eat and drink. He told them that after he was gone they should continue to observe this supper, for forgiveness of sins and in remembrance of him.

Ever since that night, the followers of Jesus the world over for almost two thousand years have observed or celebrated the Lord's Supper as their most solemn act of worship. The Holy Spirit has used this simple meal to give the church some of the most profound and richest truths and gifts of God.

When we come to the Lord's Supper, we come to remember him. We recall who Jesus is and what he has done, what he continues to do and what he yet will do. He is not visibly with us as he was with the disciples that Thursday evening. As we remember him we dwell on his life, from his birth in Bethlehem to his ascension. And what a rich store of memories that is! We remember especially the cross, where his body was broken and his blood was shed for us.

Whether we see him or not, our risen and ascended Lord is here in a living presence. He is with us, singularly in bread and wine, his body and blood. We not only have a memorial; we have a presence.

And in the bread and wine he gives us himself. This is the good news of the gospel in visible form.

It is therefore called a *Communion*. Receiving life with him and in him, we are in fellowship with him, and through him in fellowship with each other. We are reconciled to God and to each other. We are the restored family of God.

Whenever and however we receive him, we come in repentance and faith. We come to receive the forgiveness of sins. We come in penitence, in sorrow for the sins that grieve him. And we come in glad confidence that he forgives us, as he has promised to do.

The three great branches of the Christian church—the Eastern (Orthodox), the Western (Roman Catholic), and the Protestant—have developed their several liturgies around this simple meal. The Holy Spirit has enabled the churches to gather together in this supper some of the most soaring motifs of the Christian faith.

In using bread and wine, which in his day were the most common food and drink, Christ in a sense ennobled his whole creation—the stuff we see and touch and smell and taste. Both matter and spirit are his. He brings the world of matter into the service of the Spirit.

It is a sacrament of joy. The beginning and the end of the gospel is joy. The angel announced Jesus' coming as the coming of joy into the world: "For behold, I bring you good news of a great joy" (Luke 2:10). And as Jesus left this world, his disciples "returned to Jerusalem with great joy" (Luke 24:52).

It is a sacrament of thanksgiving, called the *Eucharist*. When a Christian stands before the throne of God, when all sins are forgiven, all joy restored, then there is nothing left to do but to give thanks. Thanksgiving is our only full and real response to God's creation, redemption, and the gift of heaven.

The sacrament is a foretaste of the great feast in heaven. We are already lifted up into the eternal company of "angels and archangels and all the company of heaven" as we come to the Lord's table.

All the motifs of the faith, like melodies in a great symphony, are brought together in the sacrament—repentance, faith, forgiveness, joy, love, hope, and thanksgiving!

Am I not forgiven and made one with Christ through his Word without the sacrament?

Yes, and it is also his Word, his promises, that make the Supper a sacrament. Otherwise it would be just simply bread and wine. But with his Word, in, with, and under the bread and wine, we receive Christ's body and blood. God reinforces his promise by something solid that we can see, touch, eat, drink, and taste. It is as if a person promises you $100, and then gives you his personal note for $100. He reinforces his promise with paper and ink, something you can see and touch. The Lord gives us himself in his Word and in bread and wine.

Is the Lord's Supper for everybody?

No, only for the followers of Christ, they who confess him as Lord. And, unlike the Sacrament of Baptism which is given even to babies, those who share this sacrament should be old enough to understand our Lord's invitation and promise and to desire the blessings of the sacrament (see 1 Corinthians 10:16).

Should we come often?

The Lord's Supper is God's gift to us to strengthen our faith. The Christian who realizes this will want to receive this gift often, probably as often as it is offered.

Some churches celebrate it more often than others. It has been the custom in some congregations to have Communion only on festival occasions like Christmas, Easter, and Pentecost. In others it is celebrated every Sunday. No matter how often, communicants should prepare their hearts by careful self-examination and by prayer. The Scriptures warn against coming casually as a matter of form without repentance and without faith in the Lord's promise of forgiveness.

Don't I have to clean up my life before I come?

If by "clean up" you mean getting rid of all sinful desires and habits, no. The sacrament is given us precisely to help us overcome sin. Of course, a person whose life is an open defiance of God's will, who has no sincere intention or desire to change, should not come;

it would be an insult to God to come, and would only bring further judgment upon him or her (1 Corinthians 11:29).

If the rest of my family doesn't come, should I?

Yes, but you should be careful not to stand in judgment over against them. The meal is not for the Jones family or the Johnson family. It is for each person who feels or recognizes a need for the mercies of the Supper.

Should we have the Lord's Supper at a picnic?

Probably not, unless it is a worship occasion for the congregation. Communion does not belong to an individual or small groups, but to the church to be used in its ministry. Any celebration of Communion should be within the best practice of your church.

Communion seems to be such a solemn and sad affair. Should it be?

It should be solemn. It is a serious meal, where we come with our sins to have them forgiven. But it should not be a sad affair, because we receive forgiveness and are drawn into communion with the Lord who is the source of deepest joy. We celebrate our life with him.

For reflection

1. Read Matthew 26:20-29 and John 13:1-20 and consider how what took place that night gives added meaning to the Last Supper.

2. How do the words spoken in the Sacrament—"for you"—strengthen your faith?

OTHER RESOURCES FROM AUGSBURG

A Contemporary Translation of Luther's Small Catechism, Study Edition
0-8066-0026-8

A new translation of Luther's explanations along with other catechetical study helps, such as prayers, worship rites, and Luther's introduction. NRSV and Lutheran Book of Worship texts are used for the wording of the Ten Commandments, Lord's Prayer, Apostles' Creed, and the included worship rites.

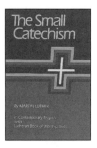

The Small Catechism in Contemporary English/LBW Texts
0-8066-1076-X

English version, Spanish version also available.

Gift Edition of Luther's Small Catechism
0-8066-4282-3

A Great Confirmation Gift! *Luther's Small Catechism, Gift Edition* is a beautiful and elegant edition of the Wengert translation of *Luther's Small Catechism* (1995). The study edition that includes the Revised Common Lectionary providing a link to the worship life of the church at large.

The Small Catechism, Downloadable Version
6-0001-7379-2

**To order, call 1-800-328-4648 or go to www.augsburgfortress.org.
In Canada, call 1-800-265-6397 or go to www.afcanada.com.**